GREATER EXPECTATIONS

ENABLING ACHIEVEMENT FOR DISADVANTAGED STUDENTS

IAN WARWICK AND ALEX CROSSMAN

GREATER EXPECTATIONS
ENABLING ACHIEVEMENT FOR DISADVANTAGED STUDENTS

CORWIN

1 Oliver's Yard
55 City Road
London EC1Y 1SP

CORWIN
A Sage company
2455 Teller Road
Thousand Oaks, California 91320
(800)233-9936
www.corwin.com

Unit No 323-333, Third Floor, F-Block
International Trade Tower Nehru Place
New Delhi 110 019

8 Marina View Suite 43-053
Asia Square Tower 1
Singapore 018960

Editor: James Clark
Assistant Editor: Esosa Otabor
Production Editor: Neelu Sahu
Copyeditor: Sarah Bury
Proofreader: Genevieve Friar
Indexer: Cathryn Pritchard
Marketing Manager: Dilhara Attygalle
Cover Design: Wendy Scott
Typeset by KnowledgeWorks Global Ltd
Printed in the UK by Bell & Bain Ltd, Glasgow

Library of Congress Control Number: 2023944897

British Library Cataloguing in Publication data

A catalogue record for this book is available from the
British Library

ISBN 978-1-5296-6810-0
ISBN 978-1-5296-6809-4 (pbk)

Contents

About the Authors   vii
Preface   ix
Acknowledgements   xi

1   Introduction: A New Narrative of Achievement   1

2   What Do We Mean by Educational Disadvantage?
And How Can We Combat It?   15

3   The Curriculum as a Source of Social Mobility   29

4   Ten Challenge Strategies to Achieve Academic Excellence   43

5   How Do We Ensure that Teaching is Always as Good as It Can Be?   57

6   Making Scholars Feel Safe and Supported   73

7   Greater Expectations: Student Destinations   91

8   Exploring Our DNA of Partnership Working   107

9   Fifteen Strategies to Drive 'Greater Expectations'   125

Afterword   139
Index   141

About the Authors

Alex Crossman is Headteacher of the London Academy of Excellence, the highest ranked sixth form provider in England to offer a full A Level curriculum. Alex's career in education has included being a Deputy Head at a sponsored academy in Brixton, the founding Head of one of London's most popular free schools and the Chief Executive of an education consulting firm based in the Middle East but operating worldwide. Teaching is Alex's first calling but his second career. Previously, he was a managing director with global responsibility for strategy at one of the world's leading financial services firms. Alex is a trustee of Reach South Academy Trust and a board member at the Eton College Centre for Innovation and Research.

Ian Warwick was originally a teacher in inner city London for over 20 years, before he founded London Gifted & Talented in 2003 as part of the groundbreaking London Challenge, which reported directly to the Prime Minister's Office, and transformed education across the capital city. Ian has written five books on more able and Disadvantaged education and has spoken at well over 150 international conferences. He has worked directly with hundreds of networks of schools and universities in countries across Europe and Africa, the Middle and Far East, to improve their provision and attainment. Ian is the Head of the Education Committee at the London Academy of Excellence and a founding member of the Eton College Centre for Innovation and Research.

Preface

The origins of the London Academy of Excellence lie, rather oddly, in the decision each of us took in our two very different schools to introduce Mandarin as a core part of the curriculum. Press speculation as to which school was first to make the move to Mandarin brought us together, each becoming a governor in the other's school. That was back in 2008.

The partnership that ensued led us to wonder if it might be possible to recreate the very best elements of an independent school in a new, free school in Newham, targeting pupils from socially Disadvantaged backgrounds. We decided early on that the greatest gap in provision was in sixth form education, and believed that, with the right partners, we could create an academically ambitious sixth form college that would bridge the gap between the many very good 11–16 schools in the borough and access to the leading universities in the country. We also believed that we must make explicit provision for a meaningful co-curricular programme, developing the soft skills that employers were (and still are) crying out for.

The name we chose reflected our ambitions. We were not to be the Newham Academy of Excellence but the London Academy of Excellence. We wanted all of London to notice us because we were convinced that we could be a model for others to emulate. And, obviously, we had to be an Academy of Excellence. Very early on, local Year 11 pupils asked us why football clubs had academies of excellence for aspirational young players but there was no equivalent academy of excellence for aspirational young academics. And so, the London Academy of Excellence was born.

Ten years on, thanks to the support of independent school partners, corporate and private sponsors, an immensely talented staff body and two outstanding Chairs of Governors, we look back with some amazement and huge pride that the vision we had all those years ago has been realised in full. The LAE is one of the leading schools in the UK; it outperforms almost every independent school in the country; and, most importantly, it is transforming young lives across East London.

We are both enormously grateful to everyone who helped to make this possible and hope that this publication will play a part in helping others to consider how the LAE model might transform the educational landscape in other parts of the country.

Richard Cairns,
Headmaster, Brighton College

Joan Deslandes OBE,
Headteacher, Kingsford Community School

Acknowledgements

This book sets out to document the extraordinary education enjoyed over the past decade by hundreds of young scholars attending the London Academy of Excellence. Those young people have been, and remain, active agents in the school's development, as in their own. No book could ever pay adequate tribute to their extraordinary resilience, solidarity, appetite for learning, and commitment to service. They remain our inspiration and it is to them that we owe our greatest debt. The future is in better hands than our own.

1
Introduction: A New Narrative of Achievement

Poverty can cast a long shadow over a learner's life. Unaddressed, disadvantage blights the aspirations of individuals, families and communities. Unchallenged, the same students slide down the same slope towards failure in region after region, generation after generation. Nationally, successive reports offer up a bleak picture of under-achievement and unfulfilled potential (Ofsted, 2013, 2015; Reay, 2017; Crenna-Jennings, 2018; Jerrim et al., 2018; Montacute and Cullinane, 2018; Sutton Trust, 2022). They reveal that thousands of our most able secondary-age children are still not doing as well as they should simply because they are poor. The stark headlines make for bleak reading. Only 16% of students eligible for free school meals (FSM) attend any university, compared to 75% of students who are privately educated, and FSM-eligible students are 100 times less likely to attend Oxbridge than someone who attended a private secondary school. These reports all demonstrate that far too few bright students from lower-income homes reach their academic potential. Even in the most effective schools, where barriers limiting the achievements of Disadvantaged students are reduced, poverty of aspiration can ensure that those reaping the greatest benefit will still be from affluent groups. Far too many Disadvantaged students are set adrift in a sort of educational doldrums from which they may never recover.

Over recent decades, the Disadvantaged educational agenda has become, to borrow Shakespeare's metaphor from *The Winter's Tale*, a feather for every wind that blows. Policy pledges to narrow attainment gaps and increase social mobility have become a much-stated standard aspiration for governments of all political

persuasions. The 1997–2010 Labour Government launched the academies programme in an attempt to unleash creative potential in the schooling system and to
bolster it with private capital in order to combat disadvantage. For the same reason, the 2010–15 Coalition Government made academy status the norm for secondary schools in England. Today, the same is becoming true for primary schools.
The Coalition Government also introduced the idea of Free Schools, new academies with substantial sponsorship from civil society groups, which, again, were
intended to target areas of high disadvantage and underachievement. The same
rationale recurs in the 2019 Conservative Government's 'Levelling Up' agenda.
This is to say nothing of the more than two decades' worth of initiatives arising
in specific cities or regions or those generated by the schooling system itself. But
progress towards these ends has been geologically slow. At current rates of progress, it has been estimated that it will take 560 years to close the 'disadvantage
gap' in GCSE attainment, not to mention university admissions (Hutchinson et al.,
2019). There is a real and growing danger that a simple, depressing narrative—
poor kids underachieve—becomes accepted as almost inevitable, a given.

The London Academy of Excellence (LAE) was established in Newham, East
London, in 2012, in an attempt to develop a new narrative of achievement—
one that turns the above narrative on its head. LAE's founding mission is to
seek out hardworking, ambitious young people from lower-income homes—
homes without any direct experience of university education—to provide those
young people with an education directly comparable in quality and scope to
that offered by the best independent schools, and to support them in their
efforts to win places at the best universities and entry to the most competitive
professions. In the past decade, LAE has experienced many fits and starts, several blind alleys and one or two failed experiments, but there has also been an
enormous amount of success. Prior to LAE's establishment, fewer than 40 students per year from the London Borough of Newham gained places at Russell
Group universities and only three were admitted to Oxford or Cambridge. In
under a decade, LAE alone has sent more than 1,300 students to Russell Group
universities, more than 200 students to medical schools and more than 150 to
Oxford or Cambridge. The first of those students are today doctors—many of
them serving the NHS with distinction throughout the Covid-19 pandemic—
lawyers, engineers, bankers, software developers, research scientists, management consultants, politicians, and some of them even teachers.[1] Most of these
young people were the first in their family to attend a university. Their success, and the success of others like them, provides a glimpse of the potential
still hidden in our education system. Small wonder that the government has
approved plans for new academic sixth forms based on the LAE example.

---

1   This list is far from comprehensive, nor is it an attempt to elevate these careers above a host of
    others. The examples merely demonstrate that students from modest backgrounds can go on
    to compete successfully in professions that have typically been dominated by those educated
    at independent schools.

This book explores the principles, processes and practices that have under-pinned LAE's success. We want to be fully transparent about two things from the outset. First, LAE is an academically selective school. This is substantially true of almost all school sixth forms and sixth form colleges, particularly those that focus on teaching A levels without a corresponding 'vocational' learn-ing pathway. LAE's entry requirements are far from the most daunting of any school in the country, and LAE combines academic selection with policies designed to promote social mobility, and therefore social justice. For example, LAE prioritises applicants who have been eligible for free school meals and those schooled in Newham, one of the most economically deprived boroughs in London. Over the past few years, those students have typically represented around 40% of the school's students. Contrast this with the finding that, in 2019, only 3% of grammar school pupils were entitled to free school meals, com-pared to the 15% of pupils in non-selective schools across England (Danechi, 2020). It is fair to point out that grammar schools are not equally distributed around the country, which means contrasting grammar pupils with national averages may not be a fair comparison as the backgrounds of grammar pupils may also be reflecting other local area characteristics. However, this is a con-sistent finding, echoing earlier very similar figures when comparing grammar school pupils to the non-grammar pupils in selective areas: 2.5% of grammar pupils are eligible for FSM, compared to 8.9% among the other pupils in the area (and 13.2% among pupils in all state-funded secondary schools) (Com-prehensive Future, n.d.). Giving this sort of priority to FSM students matters. Indeed, we would strongly argue that *academic selection as practised at LAE is a means of achieving social inclusion.* Nonetheless, we have too much respect for colleagues working in non-selective education to pretend that academic selection is not a part of this story. We hope to show that it is by no means all of the story and that there are learnings from our first decade that have value for schools and students of all kinds.

Second, the authors of this book are closer to being interested partisans rather than dispassionate adjudicators when it comes to LAE, to schools and to schooling in general. Alex is the school's Headteacher and Ian is a Governor and chair of the school's Education Committee. More fundamentally, we were both once working-class boys for whom the experience of university educa-tion was a pathway to fulfilling professions and rewarding personal lives. For us, placing schools at the fulcrum of academic excellence and social mobility is therefore both a professional priority and a personal imperative. We would like to believe that our investment in the particular form of education described in these pages has not come at the expense of our objectivity. Many of the chapters that follow directly draw on the experiences of LAE teachers whose professional and personal commitment to the school is no less great than our own. One of the most fundamental lessons of a rounded education is to follow the evidence wherever it should lead, particularly if that causes you to examine preconceptions. We would also like to believe that our enthusiasm for the form

of education practised at LAE will not be interpreted as an insistence that it is the *only* form of education that should be offered in schools. There are many schools and colleges around the country offering excellent vocational or other forms of professional learning. Their examples, too, should be celebrated. Our case here is narrower: We want to share how LAE has supported high-attaining young people from less affluent backgrounds to achieve well academically and socially in pursuit of impactful, fulfilling adulthoods.

What's wrong with social mobility?

Celebrated throughout the 1980s and 1990s by politicians and educationists alike, social mobility has come under fire in recent years. Serious scholars have been asking searching questions, not just about the practical extent of social mobility—whether and why it is up or down, whether it is a historical norm or a historical oddity—but also its moral salience, to what extent social mobility is a marker of a just society. For a school that is founded on the desire to advance the life chances of its students, a rethinking of the merits of social mobility should be a cause for serious reflection.

Oxford historian Selina Todd identifies social mobility as movement between classes (Todd, 2021). Classes, she observes, have been defined by social scientists primarily in terms of occupations, but by the upwardly mobile themselves in terms of differing cultural values and degrees of agency in the workplace. Movement between classes, Todd argues, was relatively widespread during the period from the 1870s to the 1950s, mostly because of the rise of a managerial salariat, but has stagnated in recent decades as that group has been able to reproduce itself. Successive governments' obsession with social mobility, Todd concludes, is more a soundbite to distract voters from increasing socioeconomic inequality.

Moving into the realms of moral philosophy, Harvard philosopher Michael Sandel has criticised social mobility as a notion that is not only illusory but regressive (Sandel, 2021). Sandel argues that, by focusing on the individual, social mobility, and the closely related concept of meritocracy, misdirects public attention from the need for structural reform to combat the more pernicious challenge of modern society: the increasing extremes of economic inequality. In practice, Sandel is merely reviving an argument first articulated by sociologist Michael Young—father of free schools' advocate Toby—when he coined the then ironic term 'meritocracy'. In both cases, the authors prefer policies designed to improve the lot of the many, even if only marginally, than to improve more dramatically the lot of the 'deserving' few.

Yale law professor Daniel Markovits takes aim squarely at the education system (Markovits, 2019). Markovits argues that education systems that are critically dependent on standardised testing—he is primarily concerned with universities in the United States—naturally advantage those groups in society with access to greater resources to prepare for those tests. He calls these groups 'the working rich': the doctors, lawyers, bankers, consultants and others who are able to afford independent schooling, tutors, music lessons, lacrosse, etc. Markovits' insight will be familiar to any teacher who has ever worked in a school serving a socioeconomically diverse student population.

Of the objections listed above, Markovits' view is perhaps the most comfortable territory for school leaders. Given the political centre of gravity in the teaching profession, most colleagues will agree with Markovits' criticism of the inequities built into developed education systems, but feel that their moral purpose is to help their students succeed—even, or perhaps particularly, *despite* the odds. Indeed, the LAE was founded on the conviction that all students, not just those attending independent schools, deserved access to the best schooling possible. The most common answer that interview candidates give when asked why they want to work at the LAE involves making a difference to the life chances of bright but poorer young people whom the schooling system typically under-serves.

Few school leaders will be phlegmatic about Sandel's call for a clear-sighted focus on inequality, but most will have made a degree of professional accommodation. Our roles are to support the aspirations of the students and communities we serve. Having impact locally helps ameliorate the impacts of want, one community at a time, but does not address structural inequality simply because we are not policy makers in that sense. Indeed, school leaders tend to be practical people who, like those who work in local government, have more faith in small-scale initiatives than in grand social projects. This is an understandable reaction, one that preserves the potential for personal activism outside our professional roles. But it is an inadequate one.

Sandel's recent work is a reminder to school leaders that our obligation towards the young people in our care is not only to allow them to overcome structural disadvantage, to provide a means of escape, but also to imbue them with a sense of social responsibility and the capacity to do more for those less able to join them on that journey. LAE students are far from unique in benefiting immensely from a wide range of opportunities to volunteer with local schools and charities as a way of building community resilience.

Todd's class analysis is in many ways the most contentious dilemma for school leaders in the UK (Todd, 2021). From the 2010s onwards, education for social mobility has typically been framed in terms of the progressive accumulation of 'cultural capital'. Todd, writing primarily from personal experience—an experience we share—of growing up in a working-class community in a period of high unemployment, is highly critical of the assimilationist narrative implied by an emphasis on cultural capital. (Whose culture has capital worthy of accumulation and whose does not?)

In the LAE context, the focus on cultural capital has an even more uncomfortable resonance: it risks undervaluing the immensely rich cultural heritage of young people from families with their roots in South Asia, the Middle East or West Africa. As one student of Indian heritage pointedly observed when discussing this topic: 'My culture includes Rabindranath Tagore and Amartya Sen. Those don't seem like signs of poverty?'

How can we, practically and while preserving our integrity, steer a course through this debate? Rather than focus on cultures as hermetically sealed, we see them as open and in constant dialogue. We cling to Michael Young's understanding of the school curriculum as an entitlement to knowledge, in which all share and which can transcend and even erode power structures (Young, 2014). This is not an easy or complete answer to a vexatious question, but it is a vantage point from which to enter the debate.

The Matthew effect?

Meeting the needs of able students can still carry with it that faint whiff of elitism, no matter where that learner may have been born, no matter what obstacles they may already have overcome. The very notion of intelligence seems to have become troublesome territory for many teachers. A focus on what works in a school for higher ability learners has conjured up a fear of the *Matthew effect* of accumulating advantage: *to those that have, more shall be given*. Nevertheless, the straightforward reality is that the very children who need some of the greatest support because they are smart but Disadvantaged are precisely the students who are most likely to underachieve. They don't get to go to the cultural events, they don't get to hear the right words spoken at home, they don't have their parents (or anyone else) helicoptering in when they start to slip and slide. They are the ones who are in danger of having their talent squandered, their aspirations abandoned and their future blighted. These students often go off the rails. As a result, these students do fail. All too frequently. And nationally, on an industrial scale. This is the core of the equity agenda. Unfortunately, the highest of ambition for our students is all too often sacrificed on the altar of fearful convenience and political uncertainty. This is the lack of justice that Johann Goethe (2013 [1796]) pointed out: 'If you treat people as they are, you will be instrumental in keeping them as they are. If you treat them as they could be, you will help them become what they ought to be.'

In schools, decisions about how smart a student might be has come to be seen as part of that process of making some children eligible (or otherwise) for the glittering prizes in life. Situation psychologists promote that the fault, or limitation on how educated we become, is not in ourselves, but in the home or the postcode we live in, the school we go to. It is thereby seen that our culture and circumstances shape our behaviour and what we make of ourselves. Using a student's background to predict the future is a version of the same thing. We know what to expect. At LAE, we recognise in our classrooms that there is no mythical middle ground to fit the average student. So aiming materials at that middle, in the hope somehow that the top and bottom ends can find their own level, and the more able create their own stretch and challenge, is a forlorn hope. The worst form of that inequality we are afraid of is to try to make unequal things equal.

As has been documented for many years now, we know that FSM students have continued to be twice as likely to have an SEN statement and are three times as likely to be excluded, but Disadvantaged children are not a homogeneous group: outcomes and experiences of education vary by many factors, including gender, ethnicity, first language, special educational needs and disability (SEND) status, family history of disadvantage and geography. All teachers at LAE believe that confronting these issues has to be about individual students, just as learning has for each of us always been a personal and an individual matter. As educators ourselves, learning has delivered us to ourselves—who we are, what we have or will become—and this is what we hope it will do for those whom we teach. When a student seems to fit the description of disadvantage and is then defined by that, there is a problem. Such students are not hard-wired to underachieve. Shoda et al.'s context principle maintains that individual behaviour cannot be explained or predicted apart from a particular situation, and the influence of a situation cannot be specified without reference to the individual experiencing it (Shoda et al., 2007). We know that addressing issues of disadvantage requires an understanding of the individual and an understanding of the situation surrounding that individual. It is all too easy, and not very productive, to say that poverty or low levels of family support explain everything. It is a combination of factors, including what happens in school, that form just as much a part of a student's culture as the language they speak at home, peer group pressures, family values and economic pressures.

The list of the realities that indicate and lie behind underachievement can appear overwhelming and we might feel that alleviating or changing any of these factors through the way we organise and deliver learning might seem beyond us as teachers. Similarly, changing the behaviours of individual underachievers requires a good deal more than simply telling them to behave differently, or covering our classroom walls with inspirational posters and expecting that as a result our disengaged students will experience some sort of epiphany which will transform their worldview and their levels of achievement. At LAE, when we perceive potential in a student, we cannot be satisfied unless we make some effort to find our way through this complex maze of interdependent variables.

In search of wider principles

One of the few positives of the Covid-19 pandemic has been a growing national recognition of the importance of high-quality public services—education very much included. More people today than at any time in the recent past recognise the essential role teachers and other school workers play in enabling society to function with any degree of normalcy. More people than ever also recognise that teachers work under exceptional pressures, many of which arise directly from the structure of our national education system—from falling (real) rates of school funding, from rising workloads, from Ofsted, from exam boards, from national accountability systems with their focus on ever-more-debatable ways of measuring students' progress. Indeed, one of the striking features of the pandemic has been the way in which public opinion has generally proven very supportive of schools, while being notably hostile towards other actors in the education system, who appeared to make schools' jobs harder rather than easier out of apparent lack of understanding of how our schools actually work. The former permanent secretary to the Department for Education, no less, has recently highlighted a chronic lack of meaningful engagement between Whitehall and schools when it comes to developing education policy (Slater, 2022).

So far, this conversation has been couched in terms of teachers' wellbeing and, to a lesser extent, in terms of the attractiveness—or lack of it—of the teaching profession to new graduates entering the workplace. We are grateful for this recognition. We hope it proves to be a 'Covid keep'. But if we are to seize the moment for a reappraisal of education as a national priority, there must also be a recognition of the impact of these pressures on *students* and, in particular, of what and how students learn in our schools. We are particularly focused on how in-school and national accountability systems can profoundly distort teaching and learning. Christine Counsell has written insightfully about the confusion of the curricular 'what?' with the pedagogic 'how'—more plainly, what should be taught versus how teaching should take place in each subject on the school curriculum (Counsell, 2016). We agree strongly with her analysis that the maintained sector has experienced a drive to find generic teaching strategies that can form the subject of whole-school—for which, read: 'inexpensive'—teacher development sessions, and, crucially, can be monitored and enforced by school leaders and inspectors operating far outside their subject expertise. And we agree that this drive has had a winnowing effect on the development of genuinely deep subject expertise among classroom teachers.[2]

The LAE's current Headteacher has conducted a rolling survey over the past decade of training teachers and school leaders. On first meeting a group of teachers in any training context, he would present a diagram showing Shulman's three dimensions of signature pedagogies, or what Shulman calls 'the dauntingly complex challenges of professional education [that] once they are learned and internalized … don't have to be [thought] about [but can be thought with]' (Shulman, 2005: 56). The three dimensions are:

- Surface structure: concrete, operational acts of teaching and learning, of showing and demonstrating, of questioning and answering, of interacting and withholding, or approaching and withdrawing
- Deep structure: assumptions about how to impart a specific body of knowledge and know-how
- Implicit structure: a moral dimension comprising beliefs about professional attitudes, values and dispositions

---

2   We should be clear that this does not amount to an argument that teacher accountability is unimportant, merely that it can be, and too often is, sought using the crudest of measures.

The *surface* structure is clearly what Counsell refers to as 'genericism'—operational acts of teaching and learning such as how to organise an information hunt, how to construct a seating plan or to hold a classroom discussion. All of these are foundational skills for any teacher, but they do not of themselves lead to academic excellence. Shulman's *deep* structure contains both the 'what' and the 'how' of the school curriculum and suggests that they are causally related. In laypersons' terms, this means *what* students are taught should determine *how* they are taught—a remarkably obvious statement that is, somehow, still controversial in some circles. The deep structure is the only one of Shulman's dimensions that explicitly links teaching strategies to the goal of mastering a specific field of knowledge or expertise. The *implicit* structure, the values that underpin education, is essential, and has received enormous national focus over the past 20 years, but, like the surface structure, it does not lead explicitly towards mastery.

This survey would then ask the attendees to estimate how much time they have spent on each of these activities over the course of their teaching careers. Over scores of training sessions, most participants concluded that they had spent between 50% and 60% of all professional development time on the surface structure. Implicit structure—the exploration of values—did reasonably well, taking up 20–30% of professional development time. School leaders, notably, spent more time on values than other groups. Few, if any participants, ever estimated that they had spent more than 15% of professional development time exploring how their own subject discipline creates knowledge or initiates new learners. For most teachers, the proportion of professional development time spent exploring their own subject and how it *specifically* should be taught was 10% or less. Most worryingly, there was a noticeable correlation between the socioeconomic context in which colleagues worked and their experience of professional development. Teachers whose practice was rooted in Disadvantaged communities across England, where educational outcomes were weakest, were *least* likely to spend time on subject-specific teaching strategies. By contrast, teachers working in grammar schools or in the independent sector were far more likely to estimate that half of their professional development focused on the ongoing development of subject knowledge and subject-specific pedagogy.

The reason this should concern us is simple: for students to achieve well academically *in any context* takes teaching that focuses on the deep structure of a subject discipline. What helps students to love a subject and to want to study it more, study it differently or study it at university? What unlocks enthusiasm for a career based on deep expertise in a particular field? The answer is always teachers with deep subject expertise. There are threshold concepts and powerful knowledge in every subject domain that only an expert teacher can deliver to students. When thinking about subject expertise, we subscribe to Michael Young's formulation that a fair, functioning education system requires both experts that focus primarily on extending their subject domain—

typically academics working in universities—and experts who focus primarily on opening up their subject domain to new entrants, typically schoolteachers. The difference between these groups should be understood in terms of their goals, not in terms of the extent of their understanding in their chosen field. It is in part for this reason that virtually the entire teaching faculty at LAE has Master's degrees and more than one-third have PhDs. It is also why the school's annual professional learning programme is squarely focused on deepening subject expertise and developing highly effective, subject-specific pedagogy. Indeed, we could go further and argue that one test of the integrity of a pedagogic method is provided by expertise developed in another domain. A teacher well-schooled in Gauss's law for gravity, for example, is unlikely to accept as credible a faddish teaching strategy without a clear basis in evidence. All this expertise takes time to acquire, time to preserve and time to extend. Small wonder that, at present, in the UK, there is little requirement for teachers to refresh their subject knowledge regularly as they move through their careers. But without this, our students' own journeys to subject mastery are likely to be damaged. No professional physicist, historian, engineer or software developer ever became so because their teachers were enthusiastic generalists who stuck close to the exam syllabus and mark scheme. This is the very definition of the *soft bigotry of lowered expectations* (Bush, 2000).

Teachers at LAE know that our job is vitally important and there are many ways we can demonstrate to our more able students that we understand and can support them: by not rewarding their second-best endeavours and ensuring feedback is only given on their best work; by encouraging bravery by taking risks ourselves in the classroom and by talking about our own less than perfect learning journeys; by anticipating likely student misconceptions, interrogating and challenging their responses and by not allowing ourselves to become the only thinker and questioner in the classroom; but perhaps most of all, by demonstrating our love for our subject.

It is sometimes easier to stretch and accelerate our more able students than it is to keep them on the journey with us. As teachers, we all sometimes forget that we have become experts in our subjects. We get used to explaining key concepts and the more difficult areas of our domains, but we neglect to explain to our students what it is that we found emotionally engaging about our subject in the first place—why we chose to study it and what we feel it is there to explain. So it is really helpful to use personal anecdotes, stories and epiphanies in our classroom to support our students to understand why it is meaningful. That includes making it clear that there are moments where we still get excited about our subject and why that happens. It also means that we should explain to students what helped us to get our subject, our own learning histories and where our sense of security and expertise comes from.

The ethic of excellence

We agree with Ron Berger that any work of excellence is transformational (Berger, 2013). Once a student sees that they are capable of excellence, that student is never quite the same. There is a new self-image, a new notion of possibility. There is an appetite for excellence. After students have had a taste of excellence, they're never quite satisfied with less; they're always hungry (Berger, 2013). There is a fear, often expressed in the educational world, about 'hothoused' students, who are intensively challenged, burning out. While this may be true in some situations, it is also true that there is a peculiarly cloying brand of teaching that treats the able learner as a highly delicate and fragile orchid who requires special tending. Therefore, to treat all of them as if they all have a similar proneness to over-sensitivities is foolish. At LAE, we see that many able students positively love the battle, the occasional intellectual dogfights. They enjoy risk (look at what else they often choose to experiment with at this age) and have far less fear of failure than their teachers. To use an analogy, the blend of fuel used for racing is tuned for the demands of different circuits, or even different weather conditions. More potent fuels give noticeably more power but that needs to be balanced against the danger of engine wear. However, it has to be acknowledged that the lack of demand made by the curriculum across much of the system is that students have far too few challenging circuits to negotiate. Put simply, the lack of ignition is a far more serious problem in UK schools than the risk of burning out. On a daily basis, schools then face students who have lowered their sights, lost commitment and ambition, and acquiesced to turgid spoon-feeding and easy successes. Students who are constantly under-challenged, are given material they have already mastered, often because of a rigid adherence to the basic core curriculum, have created boredom on a national scale (for both teachers and students).

Picking and mixing approaches to teaching and learning makes more sense, which is what we as teachers do all the time, but sadly, most books in search of the big idea tend not to do so. Our overriding hope is that other schools and sixth form colleges will find the explanations of what we do and why we do them at least interesting, and possibly as touchstones for adoption or adaption. By the end of this book, based on our experiences at the LAE, we hope to promote a sort of collective reasoning that does *not* conclude with *so here is the answer, do this and all will be well*, but rather allows colleagues to think for themselves, to rediscover, re-evaluate, recombine the ideas, theories and experiences expressed here into a more multidimensional attempt to help find individual solutions for individual learners.

References

Berger, R. (2003) *An Ethic of Excellence*. Portsmouth, NH: Heinemann Educational Books.

Bush, G. W. (2000) George W. Bush's speech delivered at the NAACP's 91st Annual Convention. Baltimore, MD, 10 July.

Comprehensive Future (n.d.) Grammar school myths: 'The reason low numbers of disadvantaged pupils access grammar schools today is because there are too few grammar schools'. *Comprehensive Future*. Available at: https://comprehensivefuture.org.uk/grammar-school-myths-the-reason-low-numbers-of-disadvantaged-pupils-access-grammar-schools-today-is-because-there-are-too-few-grammar-schools/ (accessed 23/07/2023).

Counsell, C. (2016) Genericism's children. *The Dignity of the Thing* [Blog]. Available at: https://thedignityofthethingblog.wordpress.com/2016/01/11/genericisms-children/ (accessed 23/07/2023).

Crenna-Jennings, W. (2018) *Key Drivers of the Disadvantage Gap: Literature Review*. Education in England: Annual Report 2018. London: Education Policy Institute. Available at: https://epi.org.uk/wp-content/uploads/2018/07/EPI-Annual-Report-2018-Lit-review.pdf (accessed 23/07/2023).

Danechi, S. (2020) *Grammar School Statistics*. Briefing Paper 1398. House of Commons Library. London: HMSO.

Goethe, J. (2013 [1796]) *Wilhelm Meister's Apprenticeship: A Novel*. The Classics.us ebook edition.

Hutchinson, J., Bonetti, S., Crenna-Jennings, W., and Akhal, A. (2019) *Education in England: Annual Report 2019*. London: Education Policy Institute. Available at: https://epi.org.uk/wp-content/uploads/2019/07/EPI-Annual-Report-2019.pdf (accessed 23/07/2023).

Jerrim, J., Greany, T., and Perera, N. (2018) *Educational Disadvantage: How Does England Compare?* London: Education Policy Institute/UCL Institute of Education.

Markovits, D. (2019) *The Meritocracy Trap: How America's Foundational Myth Feeds Inequality, Dismantles the Middle Class, and Devours the Elite*. New York: Penguin.

Montacute, R., and Cullinane, N. (2018) *Access to Advantage: The Influence of Schools and Place on Admissions to Top Universities*. London: The Sutton Trust. Available at: www.suttontrust.com/wp-content/uploads/2019/12/AccesstoAdvantage-2018.pdf (accessed 23/07/2023).

Ofsted (2013) *The Most Able Students: Are They Doing as well as They Should in Our Non-selective Secondary Schools?* London: Ofsted. Available at: www.gov.uk/government/publications/are-the-most-able-students-doing-as-well-as-they-should-in-our-secondary-schools (accessed 23/07/2023).

Ofsted (2015) *The Most Able Students: An Update on Progress since June 2013*. Available at: www.gov.uk/government/publications/the-most-able-students-an-update-on-progress-since-june-2013 (accessed 23/07/2023).

Reay, D. (2017) *Miseducation: Inequality, Education and the Working Classes.* London: Policy Press.

Sandel, M. (2021) *The Tyranny of Merit: What's Become of the Common Good?* London: Penguin.

Shoda, Y., Cervone, D., and Downey, G. (eds.) (2007) *Persons in Context: Building a Science of the Individual.* New York: Guildford Press.

Shulman, L. S. (2005) Signature pedagogies in the professions. *Daedalus, 134*(3), 52–59.

Slater, J. (2022) *Fixing Whitehall's Broken Policy Machine.* London: King's College London. Available at: www.kcl.ac.uk/policy-institute/assets/fixing-whitehalls-broken-policy-machine.pdf (accessed 23/07/2023).

Sutton Trust (n.d.) *Universities and Social Mobility: Data Explorer.* London: Sutton Trust. Available at: www.suttontrust.com/universities-and-social-mobility-data-explorer-rankings/ (accessed 23/07/2023).

Todd, S. (2021) *Snakes and Ladders: The Great British Social Mobility Myth.* London: Chatto & Windus.

Young, M. (2014) Knowledge, curriculum and the future school. In M. Young and D. Lambert (eds.), *Knowledge and the Future School.* London: Bloomsbury.

2
What Do We Mean by Educational Disadvantage? And How Can We Combat It?

Teachers and academics largely agree that there are steep socioeconomic gradients to academic attainment in England (Harris and Ranson, 2005). In simple terms, across the whole population, young people from poorer households are less likely to do well at school than young people from wealthier ones, and their degree of underachievement moves in lockstep with their experience of poverty. There is also a strong consensus that these gradients relate to the contrasting socioeconomic experience of different ethnic groups, although this picture is more complicated (Strand, 2021). Some identifiable groups, notably students of Chinese heritage, do better than others, even when intersectional analysis is conducted, that is, even when their families are poorer. These socioeconomic gradients to school achievement in England are steeper and the resulting gaps in attainment wider than in similarly developed countries (Jerrim et al., 2018). The gap between Disadvantaged pupils and their peers in England is equivalent to one whole GCSE grade. This places England at 27 out of 44 countries surveyed in terms of the size of the socioeconomic gap. What this means, for those at or near the bottom of the social pyramid, is worth highlighting. The same study found that only 10% of students eligible for free school meals during their secondary education achieved a grade 7 or above in mathematics—understood here as a proxy for eligibility for A-level study at most colleges, school sixth forms and sixth form schools. If there is one statistic that should constitute the insistent ringtone of impending national crisis, this is it. Ninety percent of students eligible for free school meals do not even achieve the grades needed to enjoy the option of studying A levels, and therefore of progressing to a degree course or degree level apprenticeship that would lead eventually to a professional career. It is not necessary to rob those young people of independent agency by prognosticating about how many of them should progress in this way: for 90%, at age 16, there is no credible discussion to be had.

The message that poorer students do less well than they should in our schooling system is often surprisingly difficult to land. In some quarters, no doubt, obduracy reflects regressive ideas about the causes of poverty and its relationship to the distribution of natural abilities. A disguised but certainly not invented version of this argument is: only X% of students have the innate ability to study Y qualifications or go to Z universities, with X, Y and Z all happening to intersect with the speaker's own experience and that of their children. No doubt the recent political climate, which has emphasised very different aspects of English exceptionalism, has not helped to foster reflection about this priority. But there are other forces of opposition, too, many of which would identify themselves as far more socially progressive. Meeting the needs of able students can still carry with it that faint whiff of elitism, no matter where that learner may have been born, what circumstances they may have faced or what obstacles they may already have overcome. Alex recently attended a community event in a part of England where A-level provision is in short supply. One of the loudest voices in opposition was from a local social mobility charity doing excellent work providing support for young people at risk of leaving school with no credible routes into further education or employment. There was no need to extend A-level provision locally, the charity's executive director argued, because bright local kids were already doing well. This in an area where the rate of A-level study is 17% across all students, less than half the national average.

The rest of this chapter deals with how LAE teachers and school leaders first understand socioeconomic disadvantage and then help students to overcome the barriers to learning that it presents.

Destigmatising disadvantage: Identifying and understanding need

The first step towards addressing students' needs is to identify and to understand them in depth. This requires, above all, the creation of a supportive school culture. Students must be made to feel sufficient psychological safety to disclose and to discuss barriers to their education—in the language of modern safeguarding practice, relational safeguarding, or the quality of relationships between students and between students and staff, must be excellent. At the same time, students must also feel a sense of agency in their own education, that the barriers they face can and should be overcome. The systems that underpin this culture at the LAE are discussed in detail in Chapter 6. In the remainder of this chapter, we focus on the practical tools that help frame our understanding of our students' needs and the strategies we use to address them.

As a practical step towards that identification of need, LAE has developed an Index of Need, supported by a wide range of evidence collected both before and after students are enrolled. Most school leaders, we fully appreciate, will have a mental checklist of students' vulnerability factors. That list may overlap closely with the LAE Index. In any case, the LAE school leadership firmly believes that the formality of the Index, its production and regular updating, is essential to truly meet need in a fully consistent way. 'Having a well-constructed framework for understanding students' vulnerabilities and potential vulnerabilities has nothing to do with labelling them; it just enables us to be more proactive in how we anticipate and address the barriers to progress they may face', says the school's long-serving Deputy Head Pastoral. The LAE Index is based, in part, on commonly used multidimensional poverty indices such as that produced by the Oxford Poverty and Human Development Initiative, on the rapid research evidence review conducted by the Education Endowment Foundation and, in part, on the criteria used by both Oxford and Cambridge universities to determine eligibility for their Foundation Year programmes, initiatives that are designed to combat educational disadvantage. The LAE Index includes characteristics related to the individual student and to their household, and considers students' educational journey to the school. The Index overlaps with but can't, for legal and practical reasons, be precisely the same as the oversubscription criteria that largely determine which students are able to study at the LAE. The school's admissions policy is already among the most socially progressive in the country in the priority it gives to applicants who have been eligible for free school meals and, from 2023, those who have refugee status or humanitarian protection (see Table 2.1).

The LAE Index helps school leaders to understand their students better, faster and more consistently, which are all key considerations for a sixth form

Table 2.1: The LAE Index of Need

1. Individual characteristics

Care experience	The student is, or has experience of being, in the care of a Local Authority.
Special Educational Needs and Disabilities	The student has additional needs affecting their education, including an Education Healthcare Plan.
Free school meals	The student has been eligible for free school meals during their secondary education. As a secondary factor, the duration of their eligibility may be considered.
Carer status	The student exercises (i) primary responsibility for caring for a relative with a disability, illness, mental health condition, or drug or alcohol problem; or (ii) the student exercises quasi parental responsibility for a sibling because of a lack of capacity elsewhere in the family.
Refugee status	The student has recognised refugee status or humanitarian protection in the UK or is in the UK and seeking asylum.
Experience of homelessness	The student has experienced homelessness, including living in temporary accommodation, during their secondary education.
Ethnic minority status	The student belongs to a minority ethnic group as defined by the UK national census. This may include being from a Gypsy, Roma or Traveller community.
Mental and physical health and wellbeing	A student has a physical or mental health issue requiring ongoing treatment by a professional and which, typically, will have resulted in an extended absence or period of partial attendance during secondary school.

2. Household characteristics

Family disruption	Social care is actively involved with the student's family, including through the framework of a Child Protection or Child in Need Plan.
Household income	The student comes from a home with a combined annual income of £30,000 or less.
Parental education	The student would be in the first generation of their immediate family to attend a university in the UK or elsewhere.
English as an additional language	Most, if not all, communication in the student's home is in a language other than English. One or more legal guardian may require the support of a translator to communicate with the school.

3. Experience of education

Contextual attainment	The student took their GCSEs at a secondary school with significantly negative value added as measured by Progress 8.
Mobility	The student has changed schools during Key Stage 4 or more than once during their secondary education.

school with only two (relatively short) school years to build familiarity and rapport. In some cases, they encourage school leaders to understand in greater depth factors that are considered widely in most schools. For example, there is an active academic discussion, mirrored in LAE leadership meetings, regarding the extent to which students suffer from ongoing versus episodic disadvantage. In their study of grammar school outcomes in England, Gorard and Siddiqui found that the rate at which students eligible for free school meals (FSM) participate in selective secondary schools—5.6% versus 25.6% in non-selective schools—understates their level of educational disadvantage (Gorard and Siddiqui, 2018). Grammar school students classified as Disadvantaged were disproportionately found to have 'dipped' into such FSM eligibility rather than having remained there for a significant portion of their secondary education, implying temporary family hardship rather than enduring poverty. Gorard and Siddiqui found a strong correlation between educational underachievement and the number of years a student has been eligible for free school meals. The LAE has, for many years, proactively encouraged students and their families to register their eligibility for free school meals so as to de-stigmatise that status in and around school. Alex often begins students' first assembly in Year 12 by pointing out those in attendance who have been eligible for free school meals includes the headteacher, some governors and several members of the teaching faculty. The LAE now also surveys students at the beginning of Year 12 to understand how long they have been eligible for free school meals. Asking the question has prompted other lines of enquiry that have added a depth of understanding to student context that, in retrospect, had been missing.

The LAE Index does not provide a definitive guide to those factors that can hamper a young person's education. The Education Endowment Foundation identifies three additional 'out-of-school factors' that contribute to the attainment gap between Disadvantaged students and their (generally) more affluent peers (Education Endowment Foundation, March 2022). These factors are:

- Perinatal factors, such as smoking, birth weight, breastfeeding
- Physical home environment, such as cold, damp, or cramped and overcrowded living, lack of computer or internet resources, lack of toys, lack of nutritious food, housing affordability, and homelessness or mobility
- Social home environment, such as parental psychological and physical functioning and behaviours (for example, inter-parental conflict), victimisation or abuse, attitudes and aspirations in the home, childrearing strategies (concerted cultivation, extra-curricular, authoritative parenting), lack of role model visibility, family structure, parental (mother) qualifications, adverse childhood experiences, lack of supported home learning (for example, homework), carer responsibilities, looked after children

The exclusion of these categories from the LAE Index is practical rather than philosophical. The school cannot reliably evidence perinatal factors. Any responsible pastoral system will pick up on the physical and social conditions in students' homes and the impact of both factors is captured elsewhere in the Index. Even on the more limited basis on which the LAE Index is currently constructed, in a typical year, more than 85% of the school's students will have one or more of the characteristics it identifies and more than 60% will have two or more. There is no artificial equivalence between the factors included in the Index, and the degree to which they prove a barrier to education varies significantly from student to student. In no case is biography a matter of destiny. One of the school's recent graduates arrived in the UK at the age of 15 as a refugee from the conflict in Syria. He spoke no English at the time and remained in the care of a Local Authority throughout his time at the school. He is currently studying History and Economics at Oxford. In general, however, teachers and school leaders report that parental experience of university is a strong dividing line in terms of students' preparedness for A-level study. This experiential learning is supported by Strand, who found a strong correlation between academic attainment in secondary schools and parental experience of university (Strand, 2021). The causal relationship between parental education and students' study habits is complex and open to interpretation. We are not making any strong argument here that people learn how to study at university and pass on that experience, directly or otherwise, to their children. Most LAE teachers conclude that parental experience of higher education is an indicator of students' learning behaviours at our phase of education but nothing more. Nonetheless, it is a significant indicator. According to LAE's Head of History and Art History: '*The difference* [between students whose parents have attended university and those who have not] *is clearly not that the one group is brighter than the other ... it's that the group without experience of higher education is more likely to struggle with independent study* [that is] *so crucial* [for A-level success].'

Admissions: Targeting need through student recruitment

The LAE is an academically selective but socially inclusive institution and deeply proud of both factors. What does that mean in practice and how does the school reconcile academic selection with its progressive agenda?

The school's context is crucial. The London Borough of Newham, where the LAE is located, is an unusual place. On the one hand, Newham has for many years had one of the highest rates of child poverty anywhere in the UK. On the other hand, in the past decade, Disadvantaged students in Newham have benefitted from an improving schooling system. In 2022, Disadvantaged students in Newham outperformed their more affluent peers at GCSE. This is the fertile ground from which the LAE reaps around 40% of its students in an average year. Disadvantaged students do less well, on average, in Tower Hamlets, Hackney and Waltham Forest—the next largest sources of recruitment—but the total pool of well-qualified applicants from low-income homes is significant. In each of the past five years, the LAE has received initial applications from more than 5,000 students for 250 available places in Year 12.

In practice, this means that the school's oversubscription criteria, the order in which it accepts students if it has more applicants than available places, are crucial. How do these criteria affect enrolment and ensure that the LAE does not fall into the well-documented trap that has beset much of the grammar school system of allowing academic selection to function as camouflage for social selection?

All applicants must have predicted grades that meet the school's minimum entry requirements. These entry requirements, it should be noted, are higher than for some school sixth forms, but not as high as others. Applicants require grades 7 or above in at least five GCSEs, including any subjects they wish to study at A level, and at least grade 6 in mathematics and English language. In 2023, the school added a provision for students who have identified EAL (English as an additional language) needs. Under certain circumstances, these students can be considered without the typical minimum requirement in English language.

In practice, around 3,500 students per year apply to the LAE with predicted grades high enough to warrant an offer. The school then begins to apply its oversubscription criteria. The law requires all schools to give priority to those students who are or have been in care and those with a statement of special educational needs. In the LAE's oversubscription criteria, the next source of priority goes to students who have been eligible for free school meals at any time in their secondary education.

It is worth spelling out exactly the impact this prioritisation has on the offers the LAE makes and the students it eventually recruits. There is a pronounced difference in the average prior attainment of applicants who have been eligible for free school meals and those that have not. In a typical year, that difference will be around one full GCSE grade across an applicants' best eight subjects, echoing the national picture, although at a higher average level of achievement.

Given the LAE's pool of applicants, a difference of a full grade means that most Disadvantaged students would not be within sight of an offer based solely on predicted attainment. In March 2023, the LAE made provisional offers to 488 Disadvantaged students. Only 47 of those students would have received an offer based on their attainment alone. A year later, the LAE made provisional offers to 612 Disadvantaged students, only 91 of whom would have qualified based purely on predicted attainment. In 2022, almost 50% of offers went to students who were Disadvantaged. In 2023, the equivalent figure was over 60%.

In short, the way the LAE prioritises applicants who are Disadvantaged results in a fundamentally different student population than would be the case if the school operated solely based on academic selection. Nationally, we know that *the rate of participation by Disadvantaged students in selective schooling beyond the age of 16 is a terrifying 4%*. At the LAE, it is routinely over 40%. And this is to ignore both the crudity of FSM eligibility as a proxy for household income and the multiple other factors that can prove barriers to a young person's education (see Table 2.1).

The LAE's teachers, leaders and governors are understandably disappointed by allegations that the school is highly selective, given these data. The fact that seemingly well-informed system leaders have sometimes thought it reasonable to dismiss the LAE's track record of success as solely attributable to its admissions criteria is fundamentally to have misunderstood who attends the LAE and why. This is not to argue that building a school devoted solely to the pursuit of academic excellence would be wrong; merely that this is not our aim.

There is still room to improve. The LAE, like all sixth forms, makes offers based on predicted attainment. We know that Disadvantaged students are less likely to benefit from optimistic predictions than other types of students. In 2023, the LAE introduced a reserve list so that Disadvantaged students whose predicted grades were just shy of an offer could be considered on results day if they outperform their teachers' expectations. The issue of refugee status also came into sharp focus after the 2022 applications round and will be reflected in the 2024 admissions process.

And there is the question of reach. There is no truly reliable data on the number of Disadvantaged students in East London who achieve the LAE's minimum entry criteria each year. Based on some reasonable assumptions, the school leadership believes that it is making offers to around 90% of such students in Newham and around 70% in surrounding boroughs. In 2023, the school pivoted its student outreach to prioritise those East London secondary schools with higher percentages of Disadvantaged students. But there is more work to be done to ensure that the students who will benefit most from the LAE's provision are located, and offers made.

Curriculum

A proactive diagnosis of barriers is one thing, but the real value of the LAE Index is as a guide to determining access to additional resources. This starts with the taught curriculum. The LAE is one of only a handful of state sixth form schools in England where all students study four A levels in Year 12. Many observers seem to think this curriculum decision is rooted in our commitment to academic excellence and broad-based achievement. On one level, that's true, of course. Expecting more of all students raises standards. As one responded to the school's annual student survey concluded: '*Doing 4 A Levels taught me a better work ethic … and forced me to better prioritise and manage my time.*' This is music to any headteacher's or school governor's ears. But the four A-level curriculum also serves another purpose in the battle against educational disadvantage. The LAE operates in a schooling environment characterised by a significant number, if not a preponderance, of secondary schools for students aged 11–16. Schools that send their students to another stage of their compulsory education often have a different perspective on careers education than schools that send their students directly to university or potentially into employment. Many employers are also more inclined to engage directly with schools that have older students whom they may want to employ in the short rather than the longer term. Most university outreach is directed at students who are a few months rather than a few years away from an application. Although no one would wish it, as a practical matter, this can result in foreshortened opportunities and guidance for students. Inevitably, those students who suffer most from that foreshortening are those who cannot compensate for it through family resources. '*Most students come join* [the LAE] *either with very limited understanding of the careers they want to pursue or with very fixed ideas*', says the school's Assistant Head for Personal Development. '*It's easier to deal with students who don't know what's out there or what they want to do than to deal with those who have very fixed ideas that aren't always very well informed.*'

The challenge is not one of low aspirations. The LAE is reflective of its immediate East London environment in that most students are from ethnic minority backgrounds. National studies clearly show that educational aspirations and attainment are higher among these minority groups and that all minorities now participate more in higher education than does the white majority (Crawford and Greaves, 2015; Department for Education, 2017; Fernández-Reino, 2017). There is, however, a challenge of *narrow* aspirations. LAE students show a very clear pattern of aspiration towards more established professions: chiefly medicine, but also dentistry, engineering, accountancy and the law. These aspirations, even where they are well articulated, often reflect parental influence more than student conviction. Parents' role in shaping young people's aspirations has been noted in several studies (e.g., Goodman et al., 2011; Strand, 2014; Chatzitheochari and Platt, 2019). There is nothing necessarily inappropriate about this degree of influence. It's rare that a young person aged between 16 and 18 should be wholly unmotivated by a longing for parental approval (although this longing can often be well disguised). It is also unsurprising that parents, many of whom will have experienced enduring financial hardship, should aspire for their children to work in fields that seem to offer both financial stability and social status. To the contrary, there is something quite unedifying about the middle-class commentariat's periodic jeremiads about unacceptably modest numbers of working-class Black adolescents aspiring to be ceramicists, or to work in some other 'creative' sector, entry to which is very often supported by access to family resources. Still, supportive, aspirational parents without direct experience of specific professions may not be well positioned to advise their children on how to access those professions, much less to comment on their child's suitability for them. The combination of these factors can lead to young people making sometimes inappropriate, sometimes ill-informed decisions not only about the destination to which they aspire, but also about the route to take. The LAE's coordinator for medicine, dentistry and veterinary sciences sums this up: *'It is one thing to want to be a doctor. It is another thing to believe you can only be a doctor or* [else] *you're a dismal failure. And it's another thing again to believe that the only way you can become a doctor—read: avoid dismal failure—is by studying medicine at a specific Cambridge college.'*

The four A-level curriculum is one way of combatting preconceptions like those outlined above—of keeping students' options open for longer. LAE students have anywhere between a term and a full school year to make a final decision about which of their three chosen subjects better supports their eventual aspirations in terms of degree course and/or career. And successive cohorts of students have used that opportunity well. In the most recent survey of students in Year 13, 46% of respondents confirmed that they had dropped the subject that they were least attached to on enrolment. Even in these cases, very few students said that they thought the time spent studying an additional subject had been wasted. *'It's important to get an insight into something outside of the subjects you've always been interested in,'* said one student (survey responses are anonymous). *'It kind of reaffirms your motivation to pursue a particular career.'* But almost 40% of survey respondents said that they had changed their minds and that the subjects they studied in Year 13 included a subject they had originally thought of as being 'just' for one year. In one comment: *'When I joined [the school], I was sure that I wanted to study Further Maths and I only agreed to study psychology because I needed an insurance option. By the end of Year 12, I understood that I wasn't the strongest mathematician and I didn't really like it that much, but I loved psychology. Now I'm applying to read psychology at uni[versity].'*

Of course, breadth is relative. The LAE curriculum is made up of just 15 A levels, all of which are quite traditional. Proponents of the International Baccalaureate would shudder. However, this is a deliberate measure designed to combat the soft bigotry of low expectations to which too many Disadvantaged students are subject. LAE students study those subjects that facilitate access to the widest range of university courses and that most professional organisations say they value. *The Sunday Times* annual schools survey routinely concludes that LAE students are better positioned to access a wide range of university courses than those of any school other than England's two leading maths schools, and in those cases, competitive advantage is bought by offering four A levels *in total*. The LAE curriculum will always be a work in progress. An annual curriculum review ensures not only that the content taught in each subject is as fresh and as challenging as it can be, but also that the logic remains sound for the boundaries of the curriculum being drawn as they are.

Leaving aside any technocratic or managerial consideration about which institutions show preference for some qualifications over others, the LAE curriculum is inherently aspirational. It represents what Michael Young (2014) memorably calls 'an entitlement to knowledge' that every young person has simply by virtue of being a member of society. Coupled with the LAE's institutional commitment to teaching excellence, the curriculum enables young people from Disadvantaged backgrounds to develop expertise that will support their personal and professional aspirations. The key to this development is that teachers understand the purpose and function of any subject they teach as fully as they can to help the students develop their own clarity and passion. Expertise is more than the quality and quantity of what we know. It is also hidden inside the more specialised ways of thinking that become the language of instruction that we use and share. We are obliged to be Vygotsky's 'more knowledgeable other', who is ready and willing to provide learners with the necessary linguistic fingerprint of words and ideas so that they might have the equipment they need to answer the challenging why and how questions we throw at them. Every teacher at the LAE seeks a thorough understanding of their subject and knowledge about how to communicate that understanding. We know that the quality of our teaching is likely to be one of the most important factors in how much our students learn, and without doubt we need more intellectual heft in the profession, based on the simple principle that no one can teach what they don't know.

Disadvantaged FIRST principles of pedagogy

The wider principles that underpin how curricula are developed, how lessons are planned, taught and reviewed, are explored elsewhere in this book. The remainder of this chapter is concerned with the specific strategies that LAE teachers are encouraged to employ proactively to identify and address the needs of students who are Disadvantaged. We call this approach Disadvantaged FIRST. The acronym serves three purposes: as a constant reminder that our core mission is to advance the life chances of students who are socio-economically Disadvantaged; as a handy mnemonic that colleagues can carry around to remind themselves of how learning can best be adapted to overcome barriers to learning associated with that disadvantage; and as part of our overall language for learning, so that we can meaningfully compare practice across vastly different subject domains. It is worth restating two things. First, the purpose of these strategies, individually and in combination, is to ensure that learning deficits do not develop and, where necessary, to eliminate those deficits quickly and effectively. Second, these strategies can only be understood in the context of our broader learning principles and commitment to engaging seriously with the 'deep structure' of learning. We do not say that the strategies themselves are incompatible with a different philosophy of education; only that they are presented here in a way that reflects our own.

The Disadvantaged FIRST approach aligns with the principles of Quality First Teaching and is based on evidence-based guidance from the Education Endowment Foundation (EEF) on Closing the Disadvantage Gap. The Disadvantaged FIRST approach is designed to help teachers provide the best possible learning experience for Disadvantaged students during lessons, with the aim of narrowing the achievement gap between them and their peers. The approach is grounded in the LAE learning essentials, which are a set of principles that guide teaching and learning at the LAE. The five principles of FIRST are: feedback, instruction, recognition, seating and testing. Table 2.2 sets out how those principles are interpreted and applied at the LAE.

Table 2.2   The Disadvantaged FIRST approach

Feedback	Teachers should give priority to responding to Disadvantaged students and lower prior attainers during classroom activities, as well as when marking their work. By prioritising these students, teachers can provide targeted support to help them overcome barriers to learning and succeed academically. This approach can create a more inclusive and supportive learning environment, promoting the success of all students, regardless of their background or circumstances.
Instruction	Teachers acknowledge that Disadvantaged students may not have had the same level of exposure to Standard English as their peers, and therefore refine their instructions and regularly check for understanding. Additionally, they ensure that subject domain language is formally taught, so that all students are equipped with the necessary language skills to succeed in their studies. By providing this targeted support, teachers can help to promote the success of Disadvantaged students and narrow the achievement gap between them and their peers.
Recognition	Teachers should use praise appropriately with Disadvantaged students, without differentiating between Disadvantaged and non-Disadvantaged students. Praise can be especially helpful in supporting Disadvantaged students, who may be more likely to develop imposter syndrome or low self-esteem. By using praise effectively and consistently, teachers can help to promote a positive learning environment that supports the success of all students, regardless of their background or circumstances.
Seating	Teachers reserve prime seating for Disadvantaged sixth formers, but do not necessarily keep them together. Instead, they mix students by factors such as ability, gender, and other relevant factors. This approach can help to promote inclusivity and equity in the classroom. Additionally, teachers should ensure that they have quick access to Disadvantaged students when circulating the classroom, so that they can provide targeted support and feedback as needed.
Testing	Teachers should make it a priority to question Disadvantaged students at least once during each lesson. By doing so, teachers can identify areas where these students may require additional support or clarification and provide timely feedback to help them overcome any learning barriers.

Conclusion: Leadership takeaways for combatting disadvantage

Any highly effective school must combine high moral purpose with a commitment to pragmatism. The focus of this chapter has been on the core systems, processes and strategies that the LAE uses to narrow, and often to eliminate, the achievement gap between students who are socioeconomically Disadvantaged and their more affluent peers. A significant testimony to the effectiveness of these strategies is that, in a typical school year, the A Level results of students who joined the LAE having been eligible for free school meals during secondary school are essentially the same as the A Level results of those students who did not. These strategies are eminently practical: they amount to knowing students better, fully understanding their needs, and tailoring provision to meet those needs. With appropriate adaptation, the tools discussed above can be replicated in other social contexts or even in other phases of education. Of course, their impact at the LAE comes from being embedded in a school culture that is wholly devoted to fostering equity in education and to developing young people as scholars and professionals. It is to the core of that process, the development of a truly rich and rewarding academic curriculum, that we now turn.

References

Chatzitheochari, S., and Platt, L. (2019) Disability differentials in educational attainment in England: primary and secondary effects. *British Journal of Sociology*, 70(2), 502–525.

Crawford, C., and Greaves, E. (2015) *Socio-economic, Ethnic and Gender Differences in Higher Education*. BIS Research Paper 186. London: Department for Business Innovation and Skills.

Department for Education (DfE) (2017) *Revised GCSE and Equivalent Results in England, 2015 to 2016*. SFR 03/2017, 19 January. London: Department for Education.

Fernández-Reino, M. (2017) Immigrant optimism or anticipated discrimination? Explaining the first educational transition of ethnic minorities in England. *Research in Social Stratification and Mobility*, 46, 141–156.

Goodman, A., Gregg, P., and Washbrook, E. (2011) Children's educational attainment and the aspirations, attitudes and behaviours of parents and children through childhood in the UK. *Longitudinal and Life Course Studies*, 2(1), 1–18.

Gorard, S. A. C., and Siddiqui, N. (2018) Grammar schools in England: a new analysis of social segregation and academic outcomes. *British Journal of Sociology of Education*, 39(7), 909–924.

Harris, A., and Ranson, S. (2005) The contradictions of education policy: disadvantage and achievement. *British Educational Research Journal, 31*(5), 571–587.

Jerrim, J., Greany, T., and Perera, N. (2018) *Educational Disadvantage: How Does England Compare?* London: Education Policy Institute/UCL Institute of Education.

Strand, S. (2014) School effects and ethnic, gender and socio-economic gaps in educational achievement at age 11. *Oxford Review of Education, 40*(2), 223–225.

Strand, S. (2021) *Ethnic, Socio-economic and Sex Inequalities in Educational Achievement at Age 16: An Analysis of the Second Longitudinal Study of Young People in England (LSYPE2).* Report for the Commission on Race and Ethnic Disparities (CRED). Oxford: University of Oxford.

Young, M. (2014) Address to Cambridge Assessment Network. Magdalene College, Cambridge, 25 March.

3
The Curriculum as a Source of Social Mobility

What do we mean by the curriculum? And why should we start there? Michael Young and David Lambert have persuasively argued that the curriculum is the *defining* feature of the school relative to other social institutions (Young and Lambert, 2014). Schools have many other responsibilities. Some of them, such as safeguarding their students' wellbeing, are arguably more essential, but only the taught curriculum is unique to institutions explicitly devoted to learning. What Young and Lambert mean by 'the curriculum' is not the bureaucratic assemblage of specific qualifications, but rather the programmatic combination of specific experiences that can lead to the progressive acquisition of specific types of knowledge and expertise deemed to have social value. At the LAE, the types of knowledge that we teach derive mostly from academic work conducted in universities. The value of this knowledge lies ultimately in its ability to further human progress, but, more often than not, our students experience such knowledge as a source of social and economic empowerment. Most of what we do focuses on the latter of these considerations, and we are unashamed in our pursuit of a school mission that stresses social justice. Nevertheless, wherever possible, we try to keep an eye on human progress, too.

We are on the borders of an intellectual and policy minefield here. The school curriculum has been an object of contention in England and Wales for generations. For some politicians, activists and educationists on the Left, the school curriculum is yet another battlefield in the bitter culture wars that have been reignited by Brexit. For these thinkers, the very idea of a school curriculum composed of 'canonical' literature, 'grand' historical narratives and other forms of 'official' knowledge is an artillery barrage launched by a specific social group—mostly white, mostly male, mostly privately educated—whose achievements it celebrates and whose norms it reproduces, against all others (see particularly Apple, 1979: Chapters 2 and 4; Giroux, 1979). On this reading, the official school curriculum is principally assimilationist, regarding children from anything other than the most advantaged, most Anglo-Saxon homes as suffering from a cultural deficit which the institution of the school exists to try to eliminate. This perspective should not be dismissed lightly and certainly should not be regarded as a facet of 'wokeness', whatever that might be taken to mean. Critical approaches to curriculum design remind teachers and school leaders to respect and value the cultural capital that our students bring with them to school (Akbar salehi and Mohammadkhani, 2013: 74, citing Fatheiva-jargha, 1388). Beyond this act of common decency, however, it is difficult to see how critical theory can provide the foundation for any progressive agenda that can be implemented in schools and which has the potential to address the stubborn socioeconomic inequalities that young people encounter. Indeed, it is surely regressive to suggest that schools should somehow deliberately deny less-advantaged social groups access to the knowledge that more advantaged social groups already take for granted. As Young asks, *'What are schools for if not to provide access to knowledge that children would not have if they were forced to rely … on their families, communities and workplaces?'* (Young, 2013: p3).

So, we start with the school curriculum because it is the most fundamental tool with which any school can address socioeconomic disadvantage and 'level up' educational opportunity. The school curriculum is a promise to its stakeholders, a set of pledges regarding the contribution the school will make towards a fairer, more just society. At the LAE, those pledges are as follows:

> The LAE curriculum is designed to cultivate expertise and character traits that will enable students from all backgrounds to access the most demanding, most rewarding degrees, degree-equivalent courses and professions. We want to develop academically resilient learners who are fully prepared to lead happy, productive adult lives and to contribute positively to society.

The word 'expertise' is used in preference to the still popular but mostly empty distinction between knowledge and skills, an intellectual cul-de-sac in which many English educationists have been stuck for decades. The expertise that most LAE students work so hard to acquire consists mostly, though not exclusively, in a degree of mastery of subjects and disciplines taught at universities. The focus on academic subjects is a function of the careers to which LAE students aspire; these are best agglomerated and understood in a modern use of the word 'profession' (see Chapter 8). Critics will argue against the primacy of these roles over others, but the intent speaks to our students' aspirations rather than serves as a normative descriptor for all potential readers. The school's commitment to wellbeing, to positive enjoyment of life and to service are equally part of the school's commitment to its students. Only once these curriculum objects have been stated does the statement become more descriptive, much less mention specific qualifications:

> The LAE curriculum is inherently holistic: it is built around academically rigorous A Levels and includes a wide range of co- and super-curricular activities. Running throughout our curriculum are high quality careers education, information, advice and guidance and a thorough understanding of democratic society in Britain and beyond. The curriculum foregrounds our school values of Independence, Humility, Kindness, Resilience and Respect.

Many elements of this broader understanding of curriculum are dissected in other chapters. In this chapter, we will describe how the core academic curriculum has been constructed, both practically and more philosophically, and why both matter to the mission to combat disadvantage.

The LAE curriculum overview

The A-level programme for Year 12 requires that students choose four A-level subjects at the start of the year, with guidance from LAE advisers. The logic behind including a fourth A level as part of students' core academic offer should be spelled out clearly. This is not an academic virility symbol. Most students arrive at the LAE having received, on their own account, relatively limited careers information, advice and guidance during their secondary education. Some students have firm and well-considered ideas about career goals, their next steps and the three A levels that will best advance them along that journey. Most do not. The inclusion of a fourth A level in the Autumn term of Year 12 allows students to keep their options open, delaying by up to a year the point at which they are forced to commit to a more restricted programme of study. The value of this opportunity is material. Student surveys consistently reveal that about half of students change their mind about one of the A levels they will study to examination during the course of their first year at the LAE. In some cases, those students will be able to access degree courses that might otherwise have been out of reach. Even for roughly half of survey respondents who say their choice of A levels did not change, the opportunity to study a fourth has benefits. Most students in this category say that they enjoyed studying a fourth A level and found links to other courses that deepened their understanding. Most also affirm that the workload involved, though at first overwhelming, forced the early adoption of effective study habits that helped with the successful adjustment to sixth form life.

All students at the LAE will study four subjects from the beginning of Year 12 until at least the first major assessment point in February (mock exams). At this point, each student will meet with a member of the academic team to discuss individual programmes of study. In order to reduce to three subjects following February mocks:

- the student must be consistently attaining Live grades of at least C grade in their remaining three subjects
- the student will be planning to complete an EPQ (Extended Project Qualification) or other additional extension work (e.g., a prize essay, a MOOC (massive open online course)) to enhance their university application
- the student's programme is agreed by the lead teachers of the dropped and retained subjects
- further Maths is considered a fourth option and can only be studied alongside three other A-level subjects (including maths)
- attendance and effort in all subjects will be considered when making decisions about individual study programmes
- the student will be timetabled into the library for study periods and is expected to be working on their A-level subjects or extension work during this study time

In May, all Year 12 students sit major internal exams, the results of which inform conversations about which subjects they continue through to full A level in Year 13. After major exams in the summer term, there is time in the curriculum for university entrance-test preparation as well as non-cognitive skills, university and careers preparation. For the majority, each will continue their best three subjects to A level at the end of Year 13. Students who complete our most rigorous Year 12 programme (i.e., four subjects plus EPQ at grade B and above) will be celebrated and their achievement will be acknowledged in their UCAS reference. These students are eligible for Year 13 Merit Scholarships.

With regard to the Extended Curriculum, Super-curricular and the Co-curricular programme that runs alongside the core academic courses, there is a wealth of opportunities to build independent learning, non-cognitive and employability skills. A typical Year 12 sixth former's week will include Clubs & Societies, Work Discovery, Community Outreach, Games, Duke of Edinburgh and Academic Literacy. Together these activities contribute to the LAE Diploma. The intention of the Year 13 curriculum is to qualify students for university entry, while preparing them academically and socially to make a successful transition to university life. Most will take three A-level courses in Year 13. It is expected that each student takes their best three subjects through to A level (i.e., they will drop the subject in which they achieved their lowest end-of-year exam grade). Before students are enrolled into Year 13, subject choices must be agreed with LAE advisers. Students attaining a D grade or below in any end-of-year examination are unlikely to carry through that subject to full A level in Year 13, although the typical progression model varies by subject both nationally and at the LAE. A small number may take four A-level subjects through to Year 13, subject to discussions after assessment points. In exceptional circumstances, students may be offered a two A-level programme following the end-of-Year 12 examinations, subject to agreement with the senior leadership team (SLT) and the academic team. The option of a reduced curriculum is typically only available to students whose personal circumstances have changed during Year 12 in a way that makes the successful completion of a three A-level curriculum unrealistic. Students are also only offered two A-level curricula where the school is able to identify a credible next step in education or into employment based on a reduced number of qualifications.

University preparation, intervention and revision classes are timetabled activities for all Year 13 sixth formers. The same programme of Games and Clubs & Societies is provided in Year 13. The Outreach and Work Discovery programmes are optional for Year 13 students. So, a typical week for a Year 12 LAE student will look like this: Each student has six 50-minute lessons per week in each of their A-level subjects (24 lessons a week in Year 12, 18 lessons a week in Year 13). In addition, students will have one timetabled lesson of EPQ preparation/Academic Literacy/UCAS preparation and a lesson dedicated to clubs and societies (up to 26 timetabled lessons in total). In Year 12, learners will typically have two Study Periods a week and in Year 13 four Study Periods a week. If a Year 12 student moves to three subjects from February, they will be timetabled into the library for their Study Periods. One afternoon per week is dedicated to the Games programme, which is compulsory for all students.

This section has covered the LAE curriculum overview in a very practical way in terms of student commitment and preparation. The rationale for the bigger picture of course construction, subject domains and the conceptual architecture that underpins the curriculum is explored in the following section.

What is central to the mastery of a subject?

Cognitive science leads to the rather obvious conclusion that students must learn the concepts that come up again and again – the unifying ideas of each discipline. (Willingham, 2010: 48)

Every subject has a rationale behind its construction, a legacy, a heritage which underpins it. These are the concepts that come up again and again—the 'aha' moments, the critical points when students make 'learning leaps'. In short, these are the hidden wiring of subject disciplines. Understanding and recognising the most important conceptual areas of our subjects (upon which all else rests) helps us to make better decisions about what and how to teach, and help us as teachers to strip away the dross that clogs up the curriculum. This is not a fringe argument, still less an esoteric one. The vital importance of conceptual architecture in effective learning has been the subject not only of academic research but of important policy work over the past two decades. Professor Tim Oates' ongoing reviews and refinements of the national curriculum in England and Wales, starting in 2011, emphasised the fundamental importance of concepts in learning:

> 'Organising concepts' are needed to facilitate retention in memory, develop economic mental processing, and support analytic reasoning. Concepts and principles are critical. The specific information embedded in contexts can decay into mere 'noise' unless individuals have concepts and principles to organise and interpret them ... Transnational comparisons make clear that high-performing [education] systems indeed focus on concepts and principles. (Department for Education, 2011: np)

This principle has been translated into settled practice at the LAE. As one lead teacher succinctly put it: *'We encourage all students to focus on the domain of our subject, what our subject is there to deliver and the broader insights that it provides into how the world actually works.'*

Meyer and Land call these ideas 'threshold concepts' (Meyer and Land, 2003). Threshold concepts enable learners to see a significant area of human knowledge in a fundamentally different way; they are 'portals opening up a new and previously inaccessible way of thinking about something' (Meyer and Land, 2003: 1). Put succinctly, threshold concepts encompass those differences in thought that divide the expert from the layperson. Meyer and Land refer to threshold concepts as the 'jewels' of the curriculum. If a student fails to pass through the threshold, they may not be able to progress further in a subject. It also just happens to be the aspect of a subject on which students often get stuck. Take the example of an astrophysicist mapping the galaxy by measuring light oscillations from stars to identify the gravitational field of nearby planetary bodies. The threshold concept she has mastered is that of gravity; without this understanding, no aspect of stellar cartography can be conceived or understood. Or consider the case of a historian tracing the evolution of radical activism in the Suffragette movement through police records and diary entries. The threshold concept at work is evidential reasoning, without which no scientific understanding of past societies is possible. Students—some students, at least—have always mastered threshold concepts, but they have not always been taught them. Indeed, differences in conceptual understanding in the secondary setting have often been regarded by teachers as markers of students' intelligence. Perhaps they are. But until all teachers are aware of threshold concepts and embed them into their curricula, we should not rush to judgement.

What is the nature of these threshold concepts?

It is one thing to acknowledge the pedagogical power of building the curriculum around a series of threshold concepts, quite another to identify the specific threshold concepts that actually underpin expertise in psychology versus economics versus languages. The blank page, or curriculum planning sheet, has a basilisk stare. How do we know a threshold concept when we encounter it? Meyer and Land also identify several characteristics that can be useful to classroom teachers.

The first and most significant characteristic of threshold concepts is that, as an idea, they are 'troublesome'. Often conceptually difficult, counter-intuitive or alien, it often means that our students are required to jettison former ideas to absorb new ones, and this sense of one step forward, two steps back can be emotionally challenging. The student is part way towards mastery, oscillating between old and new understanding and not yet there. The students who confidently accept this ambiguity are often said to have flair—they take risks. As a result of this acceptance of inherent difficulty, the way they choose and arrange words is more nuanced. Their reference points tend to be wider. Such confidence is often characterised by an understanding of the 'underlying game' of learning, while more vulnerable learners can remain defended, cautious, not wishing to let go of their customary way of seeing things. There is an all too understandable fear of getting it wrong, of rejection and failure. In some subjects, the troublesome nature of the threshold concept is explicit. In philosophy, for example, the notion of problematisation involves the conscious deconstruction of conventional understanding to achieve fresh or deeper insight. Science education has long had a commendable awareness of the need to anticipate and challenge students' preconceived (often intuitive) notions of how things work before introducing new concepts. In physics, for example, fields provide a cognitive schema for the understanding of forces, but require students to leave behind simpler understandings limited to attraction and repulsion. In chemistry, each key stage typically begins with a jettisoning of previously held understandings of the atom. (This last example introduces one of the ironies of curriculum conventions internationally: many of the prior understandings that must be revisited and revised to achieve genuine subject expertise are the product of prior teaching in the schooling system.)

Standardised responses and mimicked writing in the convention of the exam is a useful first step for our students, who don't have the variety of safety nets of their more advantaged peers. However, at some point this needs to be abandoned, so, in the words of one of our lead teachers, we make it clear to all students that *'you will get lost and confused, but you will also recover—so we stress that we're all meant to be feeling a little inadequate, we just couch it sensitively'*. In a significant way, this can also address issues around 'imposter syndrome'. As that lead teacher's comment makes clear, we are all imposters. We all have insecurities and uncertainties around our subject knowledge. Thus, it is fully understandable if our students suffer from imposter syndrome. But it is a temporary phenomenon. Humility matters with regard to true scholarship. Yet there is a commitment in many schools which have high percentages of less advantaged and vulnerable learners to focus on the security of marking schemes that too often are used in ways that compartmentalise and damage wider learner understanding. The reduction of learning into simplistic 'bite-sized' chunks ends up distorting subject structures, manoeuvring some exceptional learners into adopting the role of a passive follower of marking schemes. This approach tends to lead to the vandalism of distillation, a place where students feel that if they can just memorise this or that fact/quote/procedure/equation, they will demonstrate their grasp of the subject. It is a very vulnerable position for a student when mimicry can stand in the place of comprehension.

What naturally follows on from this is that thresholds are also characterised as 'transformative', offering a fresh perspective that involves a shift in understanding. An example of a transformative concept taken from the study of chemistry might be molecular geometry. Until students develop required spatial awareness and visualisation skills, they tend to learn the shapes of molecules by rote and hope for the best. But once they truly understand 'Valence Shell Electron Pair Repulsion' (VSEPR) theory, they not only understand why molecules have the shapes they do, but they are also able to predict the shape of unusual molecules. In political science, a transformative concept might be 'legitimacy', or an understanding that force alone is rarely ever a sufficient condition for political authority unless supplemented (or buttressed) by the widespread acceptance of that authority. When grasped, threshold concepts like these alter perception and lead the student into a different relationship with their chosen subject and, even more significantly, how they see themselves as a student, without which the learner cannot progress. The learner begins to think more like a professional in that discipline, and it is fundamental to the grasp of a subject. Shying away from the big ideas is always a false saving. As a teacher, if you gloss over the distinctions between key concepts because they are difficult and you fear losing the learners, you can end up distorting what you say.

As one lead teacher lamented, '*Poor generalisations, based on fear of complexity, lead to bad understandings in the form of misconceptions, which in turn then have to be unpicked later*'. This more fearful approach leads to far more uncertainty and, in the long run, a great deal of wasted time and effort. As we know, once a misconception has become embedded, it is a far harder job to try to release it. More advantaged students tend to deploy language with greater intent, as a tool for expressing precise thought, and show an acute sensitivity to exactly what the question might be asking for. Less advantaged learners often have far less experience of being asked to think within a discipline and may have been offered significantly fewer opportunities to do so. They can be stymied if required to look outside a more familiar lens of 'common sense' and as a result may struggle to invest in and rely on more uncertain, often paradoxical, and ambiguous concepts.

   A third characteristic of a threshold concept is that it is 'integrative'. It exposes a previously hidden interrelatedness of one thing with another. This represents a form of intertextuality that more advantaged learners often have at their fingertips, usually through wider exposure to cultural capital and access to more forms of concerted cultivation. Students with more uneven, spikier profiles don't yet know the extent of what they don't know. They have not been exposed to their own ignorance by teachers, perhaps through a fear of damaging fragile self-esteem. In some schools, praise, scaffolding and encouragement all too often replace rigour and challenge. Not so at the LAE, as one lead teacher noted: '*It's important to us at LAE to expose any student uncertainties, to confront all that they don't know, to help to build up their resilience. It matters far more that our students are genuinely daunted but also supported.*' When there is too little explicit interrogation by teachers of the specific views offered by their students there can be a resultant fragility to the knowledge of such learners at the edges. Attending to the long-term and indirect subject-specific knowledge is not some luxury; it is urgently necessary. This was highlighted by the lead teacher who argued: '*It is our responsibility to point out connections between subject areas and follow them up no matter how challenging students may find them.*' This focus on integrative understanding should not be misunderstood as a proxy for reductive notions of cultural capital or of the cultural constructs that some students absorb in the home environment to the benefit of their achievement in some humanities-based subjects. The steep socioeconomic gradients that exist across the curriculum are evidence that integrative understanding is required *everywhere*. To take one of the more obvious examples: students who are Disadvantaged often have a more restricted topographical experience, travelling less, even locally, in childhood and adolescence, than students from more affluent homes. This means that Disadvantaged young people studying A-level biology often lack a sense of how environments differ across Britain; often struggle to name even basic British organisms; and will need to learn from first principles how these things interrelate, including how they shape their own mental schema for biological existence.

The integrative function of threshold concepts further proves their worth. Understanding the conceptual architecture of a subject enables domain experts to acquire, organise and memorise vast quantities of information in a way that would not be possible in the absence of such a structure. In the classic research study, the American psychologist Herbert Simon, demonstrated that chess grandmasters were able to retain accurate impressions of tens of thousands of logically sequenced attacking or defensive formations but were no better than novices when it came to memorising pieces that had been scattered around the board at random (Simon, 1973). In the same way, an accomplished rock guitarist will use pitch axis theory to play 'Satch Boogie' with a high degree of accuracy, but is unlikely to be able to remember all the notes if asked to list them. In both cases—and many more—what we refer to as expertise is really the sum of a series of mental models developed to solve specific problems and imprinted on the long-term memory.

Threshold concepts may also be 'bounded' or restricted. In the literature, boundedness is often associated with a discipline's special language, which can be illustrated through the use of specialist terminology that acquires a meaning in one subject that can clash with more everyday usage. One example is to explore how many scientific words are used in different ways. Some are common, such as cell; others more specialist, like cytoplasm. Some words are very similar to each other but mean different things, such as 'skin' or 'membrane'. Some words, for example 'tissue', have a distinct meaning in science and another in everyday English. We also need to be careful in reading language that relates to learning in science, such as 'variable' or 'sample size', as these words have specific implications, often with a technical meaning or process attached to it. These seeming contradictions often lead to more questions than answers, and therefore point towards new conceptual areas that may not seem to be finite or fixed. Here is how a lead biology teacher thinks about her subject:

A great lesson is not just spec points-on-the board. It involves intense discussion between students, always using the language of biology, to reach independent conclusions and to make original connections about how the biological world functions. Students who are immersing themselves linguistically in biology will more naturally be able to relate biological principles to the wider world, whether that's through practical experiments or just by making the mental leap to their own experience.

Unfortunately, there are many Disadvantaged and vulnerable students who don't get to hear anything of this type of necessary academic vocabulary either at home or in the playground. It is the source of a great deficit. Knowing about an idea is powerful, but only if it can be expressed and communicated virtuously and concisely, with consideration and respect. There is a direct line from Aristotle's account of virtue to Grice's cooperative principle: to answer something well is to answer to the right degree, at the right time, for the right purpose, and in the right way. It is important to teach learners who may well have previously achieved good grades at GCSE through rote memorisation and regurgitation of marking schemes, about the impact of addressing such difficulties in language. Words and meanings don't always match. Language doesn't stand firm. The linguistic universe is in a state of continual flux. So, it is vital that teachers use the specialised language of their subject in all of its nuanced complexity, until such vocabulary feels comfortable and becomes so second nature that learners can confidently move about within it. This in turn can help to minimise the danger of learners relying on spotting features, or falling back on predictable responses, and drilled analysis rather than a more instinctive understanding of the language of the discipline. To increase the level of challenge is significantly bound up in the way we immerse our students in the language of our discipline, the language we model and the language we encourage them to read, write, speak and think in. By raising the quality of language used in the classroom, we can simply and effectively raise the challenge. Another lead teacher put it like this: *'So the direction of the course is key—established through wider concepts and integrated assessment objectives—as that helps to establish perspective on our subject and typical discourse and dialogue. That in turn establishes what's distinctive about our subject, such as flexibility, context, artefact and, critically, voice.'*

Once a student has fully grasped them, threshold concepts are also seen as 'irreversible' in the sense that they are difficult to unlearn. While there is no simple passage in learning from easy to difficult, threshold concepts represent significant crossing points, even rites of passage. A student who has learned to differentiate between statistics and mathematics will never confuse the two again. A student who has understood the importance of provenance will never again read literally a document, speech, photograph or newspaper cartoon. One who has understood hermeneutics will never again see an identity between the author's intent and the reader's interpretation. What is often overlooked in teaching English literature, for example, is that writers have a box of tricks that they can use to create impact. It is important to recognise that how something is written is far more significant than what it is seemingly about. Through close analysis of many differing texts, a threshold insight can be gained into the processes of writing itself, the nuts and bolts, the craft. Only when we make these skills and techniques visible can students learn from them, understand inference, engage with substantially more complex texts, and hopefully begin to create their own as well. Once they have seen that any text is simply a construct, a clever deceit, they never look back. Every new text they encounter will be viewed through this lens. A lead teacher widened this point by commenting that there aren't any shortcuts to understanding and that students, *'can only fully understand a discipline through immersion and investment. It is a serious mistake to believe that the most challenging aspects needed to achieve the very top grades in exams can be taught in isolation'*. When they are, they feel tagged on, and consequently learners tend to present as less assured, often appearing inauthentic. Such learners can also become far more reliant on extraneous activities and efforts to 'engage' them, rather than investing in the subject itself. In this sense, practice does not make perfect, it makes permanent. It is important to teach learners who may well have achieved good grades through rote memorisation, about the impact of desirable difficulties and liminal learning. It is also worth mentioning here that a poorly adopted proxy or default position is often mimicry, where real understanding is substituted with ritualised performance, with students being required to take refuge in reciting knowledge rather than using it. For many reasons, more advantaged learners often reach these subject-specific frontier moments earlier in their academic trajectory. As a result, they tend to demonstrate greater ease, speed and confidence in their arrangement of material and can express their judgements more clearly when required. Going through these frontier moments and gaining an insight into how a subject looks and feels does not mean everything falls into place. Sometimes it is the opposite. But it does place students in a position where they can see the complexities of a domain for themselves. It then becomes the job of teachers to highlight the difficulties and not to shy away from them. This is succinctly summarised by this lead teacher's insight: *'We're open with the students that there are texts that they—even the strongest students—probably won't fully understand yet. And that's okay: Complete, settled understanding isn't the norm in our subject, and ambiguity and uncertainty are in themselves profoundly useful qualities.'*

Why do these threshold concepts matter?

Central to all the above is the need to develop our students' conceptual understanding across the range of subject disciplines that we teach. There is a growing consensus among educators at all levels, from early years to higher education, that the process of learning is most rapid and, perhaps more importantly, learning gains most robust where teachers focus on the development of conceptual understanding.

This principle is mirrored in the LAE's subject leads' understanding of their responsibilities as educators: *'We build in opportunities to go well beyond the specifications, so that our students are grounded in the wider universe of our subject and not just that part that they happen to cover for their A level.'* This is an approach that has had success is for subject leads to address with departments where the conceptual 'knots' are in their subject. What are the bits that give the most trouble when we are communicating them to our classes? These will usually be threshold concepts as many of these ideas are intrinsically complex and student progress will therefore be messy rather than smooth and linear. It is important not to deny students access to ideas just because they might take time to click into place, or may result in confusion.

As threshold concepts are those big ideas that give a subject discipline its coherence and integrity, their mastery is key to thinking like an expert in any subject. A systematic understanding of threshold concepts offers something more: the prospect of designing our progression models around a sequence of opportunities to precisely master these concepts. Indeed, the enquiries that underpin such schemes of learning should be explicitly targeted at developing such mastery. The tricky or knotty concepts that underpin our subject need to be offered to students in a form that doesn't short-circuit their own thinking.

Conclusion: Leadership takeaways for developing the curriculum

Despite decades of often contentious policy work, the school curriculum remains, paradoxically, under-theorised and under-explored specifically in its role as a fillip for social mobility. In part, this state of affairs reflects a preference for add-ons or substitutions when it comes to curriculum content, rather than for reframing core components of the curriculum so that they better serve the requirements of a proper epistemic apprenticeship. If we want students from all backgrounds not only to 'think like' engineers, architects, doctors and diplomats, but actually to *become* all of these things, we need to start from a position of authenticity; not shying away from complexity but painstakingly building the mental models that underpin genuine expertise in any subject domain worthy of the name. There is a common misapprehension that academic debate within a subject, however profound, is a barrier to an understanding of its deep structure. This is to take the argument about concepts to its epistemological breaking point—or evaporation point?—far removed from anything that can inform school activity in pursuit of a progressive social agenda. In practical terms, the threshold concepts that make up our subject domains are often open to interpretation, less commonly to ontological dispute. For example, sociologists from different schools will dispute the nature and construction of knowledge but tend rarely to challenge the idea that knowledge itself is a core focus of sociological enquiry. Only when our curriculum leaders are clear on the conceptual structure of their subjects can we talk meaningfully about the pedagogical strategies, systems and processes that best support their progressive mastery by our students—in Counsell's terms, the *what* must precede the *how* (Counsell, 2016). The what must also directly inform the how. It is to that relationship between curriculum and pedagogy we now turn.

References

Akbar salehi, and Mohammadkhani, K. (2013) The school curriculum as viewed by the critical theorists. *Procedia – Social and Behavioral Sciences, 89*, 59–63. https://doi.org/10.1016/j.sbspro.2013.08.809

Apple, M. (1979) *Ideology and Curriculum* (2nd edition). New York: Routledge & Keegan.

Counsell, C. (2016) Genericism's children. *The Dignity of the Thing* [Blog]. Available at: https://thedignityofthethingblog.wordpress.com/2016/01/11/genericisms-children/ (accessed 23/07/2023).

Department for Education (DfE) (2011) *The Framework for the National Curriculum: A Report by the Expert Panel for the National Curriculum Review.* London: Department for Education. Available at: www.gov.uk/government/publications/framework-for-the-national-curriculum-a-report-by-the-expert-panel-for-the-national-curriculum-review (accessed 09/08/2023).

Giroux, H. (1979) *Theory and Resistance in Education.* London: Heinemann.

Meyer, J. H. F., and Land, R. (2003) Threshold concepts and troublesome knowledge: linkages to ways of thinking and practising within the disciplines. In *ISL10 Improving Student Learning: Theory and Practice Ten Years On* (pp. 412–424). Oxford: Oxford Brookes University.

Simon, H. (1973) Perception in chess. *Cognitive Psychology, 4*(1), 55–81.

Willingham, D. (2010) *Why Don't Students Like School?* San Francisco, CA: Jossey-Bass.

Young, M. (2013) Overcoming the crisis in curriculum theory: a knowledge-based approach. *Journal of Curriculum Studies, 45*(2), 101–118.

Young, M., and Lambert, D. (2014) *Knowledge and the Future School.* London: Bloomsbury.

4
Ten Challenge Strategies to Achieve Academic Excellence

The wider UK picture for challenging more able students

There is an evocative and instantly recognisable phrase to describe the UK's (and no doubt many other nations') national obsession with grade boundaries, levels and league tables. The phrase is *anxious literalism*. It implies that schools work with such a frantic level of conscientiousness that they can effectively install a glass ceiling over learning. Teachers can tend to teach to the tests and worry when students do not seem to be working at the required or predicted level. There is a danger that we forget individuals; we think of them as a limited set of scores and anything outside that we treat exactly as we would a typo. The truth is that no student can be reduced to a couple of test scores, but in our anxious literalism perhaps we sidestep the very top-end students because they will get there anyway, won't they? If the learning environment we provide does not accommodate individuality, then every aspect of that student's performance will be constrained. If we neglect the excitement and potential for immersion that might convince students that learning is worthwhile and that they might benefit from studying a subject further, we need to teach beyond exam requirements and explore the core ideas that make sense of our subject.

It can be difficult for able students to genuinely understand what excellence and scholarship might look like, for them to appreciate what a subject explains or offers to the world, if teachers insist on feeding them only bite-sized, easily digested chunks. We need to talk explicitly about subject mastery and not gloss over the big issues and complex concepts in our subject. Learners are *experts in development* and we have to come clean about the fact that becoming an expert is about challenge and struggle. We don't have to spell this out in mini-lectures or inspirational posters on the wall; we simply have to model high-level immersion in the subject-specific language we use in our teaching—by avoiding synonyms and dumbing down. When we are clear in our expectations regarding the accuracy and precision of the technical language we use, we are making it clear that precision is expected and feeds a higher level of thought and debate.

Across schools nationally there is an acknowledged variability to the extent to which expectations, assessments and tasks challenge students to learn. As noted by Ofsted, the UK appears to have developed a squeamishness about recognising and developing high-ability students. In reality, Ofsted did their best to keep challenge and high ability on the school agenda and to focus on how much of the teaching experienced by the more able students often results in lacklustre progress. In two thorough reports, in 2013 and 2015, they pointed out that the most able students are not achieving anywhere near as well as they should, that there is too little focus on academic excellence and that students get used to performing at a far lower level than they can achieve (Ofsted, 2013, 2015). The Chief Inspector of Schools at the time of these reports, Sir Michael Wilshaw, said that what they found painted a bleak picture of underachievement and unfulfilled potential. The reports also highlighted that how more able students experience their schooling is a touchstone, or an indicator, of how well or otherwise schools meet the needs of all children. There isn't a consistent commitment to strive for excellence. Rigorous high standards to enhance student learning are also not consistent. There is a lack of challenge that ironically may well have the impact of increasing student dependency. Ofsted found that teachers need to more consistently model expertise through exceptional subject knowledge, clear instruction, engaging explanations and examples, and sophisticated questioning.

Students' learning needs to be better sequenced cumulatively to build knowledge and understanding, including by 'front loading' the most challenging content; through regular, planned retrieval practice; and by signposting links between current, prior and future learning. Students need to be consistently challenged to think hard about the most transformative ideas in their chosen subjects and to develop understanding beyond the specification and into undergraduate study.

What are the difficulties we need to address?

Some of the issues that regularly arise in schools need to be more openly acknowledged, such as students who avoid having to engage with difficulty by seeking help immediately and who are reluctant then to make mistakes. For them, there is a tendency not to talk back to, negotiate with or question teachers and to assume that the teacher's job is always to be on hand with answers. They can seem fearful of being seen as less than smart, and can be defensive with feedback and resentful being exposed to what they don't know.

There are many students who don't really listen well or value each other's views or ideas and often don't take notes unless directed to do so. When asked to feedback, it is common to see students simply offering and adding generalities and opinions without feeling the need to justify or support their answers or to weave their ideas into a more complex argument. The students seem more interested in marking schemes or their own result than in any explanations or suggestions for deeper learning that their teachers might offer.

In conversations with hundreds of teachers, they have often noted that many students avoid extended writing tasks and find it difficult to manage a range of ideas and perspectives. They won't read around the subject unless specifically directed to do so, and even then often seek to do only the bare minimum. They often stick rigidly to the demands of the syllabus only, seek shortcuts wherever they can and may question teachers who stray off that perfectly paved path. They tend to prefer the comfortable relearning of familiar information rather than trying to recast material to own and master it. They often hide from mistakes, or ignore or quickly correct them rather than studying and learning from them. They don't feel the need to seek out expert feedback to develop their performance and are poor at offering peer feedback. They don't seem to understand that easy and mechanical practice leads to both interview and exam meltdown.

Ten strategies used at the LAE that address some of these issues

1. Develop courses based on threshold concepts that explore the core of a subject

Demonstrating to our students that bite-sized approaches distort learning

As LAE teachers we always go to the marrow of the subject—where the excitement sits—and then rein it back in. Start lessons and schemes of work with questions that are much harder than the students could ask themselves. That leads them into that curious place where they want to know what happened next, to further push the boundaries within and by themselves.

Focus on the knowledge that yields the greatest cognitive benefit, learning the concepts that come up the most, the unifying ideas of each discipline. Focus on the big ideas that give a subject discipline its coherence and integrity; their mastery is key to thinking like an expert in any subject. A systematic understanding of threshold concepts offers something more: the prospect of *designing our learning pathways around a sequence of opportunities to precisely master these concepts.* Indeed, the enquiries that underpin such schemes of learning should be explicitly targeted at developing such mastery. The tricky or knotty concepts that underpin our subject need to be offered to students in a form that doesn't short-circuit their own thinking. They can also be transformative, offering a fresh perspective that involves a shift in understanding. It alters perception and leads the student into a different relationship with their chosen subject and how they see themselves as a student, without which the learner cannot progress. Shying away from the big ideas is always a false saving. Glossing over the distinctions between key concepts because they are difficult and because there is a fear of losing the learners can end up distorting those ideas. They need to be offered in ways that don't compromise their integrity and their challenge. Accept that as many of these concepts are complex, progress may well be messy rather than smooth and linear. But the focus on them will help courses to focus on the necessary core, and to strip back content and be less dependent on the constant changes to the curriculum. We must take the stabilisers off and counteract the tendency of students to want everything spoon-fed and 'bite-sized'. Students need to get that such compartmentalised and *simplistic chunks of content can vandalise and distort subject structures* and push them into adopting the passive role of a follower of examination marking schemes that in turn reduces or damages their wider understanding.

2. Clarify the purpose and relevance of your subject to establish greater engagement

Establishing for our students what our subject is there to do in the world

More Disadvantaged students need far more focus on why *they are learning something—what the point of studying Ethics, for example, might be, especially when it doesn't immediately fit with their world view or environment. So every lesson at the LAE has a clear purpose—and our students must be clear about the 'why' they are learning as well as the 'what'.*

We often make a classic hindsight bias assumption when we believe that it will be obvious what function our subject performs and what delights it contains for future study. By focusing the courses on what our subject gives and what it is there to explain or offer, we allow greater student autonomy. In any learning environment students need to have these explicitly explained so that they can make the emotional leap necessary to engage fully with what and why we are teaching them. All able students comment that they want to know why things are studied and where their learning is going next. *Establishing the 'why bother' element is key in course design*, particularly for more Disadvantaged students who will most likely focus on the sections of the course that seem to offer the greatest impact in their eyes. So *clear explanations of purpose really matter*. Present your subject ideas as live, relevant and dynamic, and stress the sense of possibility and discovery by not focusing on what is already done, dusted and certain. It is counterproductive to neglect the excitement and immersion that convince students to want to study our subject further. It is important to explore how our subject has developed over time and why changes happened when they did. Introduce early thinkers and experts whose inferred versions of reality were the currency before the current reigning narrative took over. It is vital to locate what has helped to shape our subject and show how they are part of its 'back story'. Where our subject may be going and what remains to be discovered in the future helps to establish why our students may want to further their studies in our subject area if they choose to investigate it further at university.

3. Focus on longer-term narrative arcs with clear signposting of wider learning objectives

Engaging our students with measuring their own longer-term learning

Academic expectations, as high as they are at the LAE, can also be frightening. We have learned not to moderate those expectations but to position them as opportunities [rather than burdens] on a long path to understanding. We explain them right at the start of every course. We have them for so little time that we have to. To ascertain where they are, where they might want to be, what stands in their way. We need to explain the considerable challenges of getting into world-class universities from the very beginning, signpost what they need to achieve and the depth of thinking required to become an expert in our subject.

In many courses, too much time tends to be spent working out what students 'know' after any-and-all engagements. For every unit or topic being developed, we need to approach long- and short-term planning with clearer ideas about how we want students to develop a genuine understanding of content and how that fits in with how they see our subject area. Sometimes this will be through single, episodic sessions and at other times it essentially needs to be developed across a series of interactions that may take several weeks. It is *a serious mistake to believe that the most challenging skills needed in exams (such as inference) can be taught in short, isolated bursts.* When they are, students tend to present as less assured, often appearing inauthentic. It can also lead them to become reliant on extraneous activities and efforts to 'engage' them. It is worth mentioning here that mimicry, where real understanding is substituted with ritualised performance, takes refuge in reciting knowledge rather than using it. We need to ensure that students *don't see learning as a series of easily obtainable learning objectives*, but rather see the wider, long-term arc of the course across a series of activities that link together across a term. The process of separating the feeding versus the weighing of the pig needs to be built in as an implicit and explicit angle throughout the course. Clear signposts need to illustrate that this is where our students are going, and by sharing explicit learning objectives with them it gives them the opportunity to measure their own learning. When framing learning objectives for more able students, it is important to make explicit what the learning will be, and to build in sufficient intellectual challenge. In the learning phase, efforts should be focused solely on developing students' subject knowledge and understanding by nurturing their intellectual curiosity through opportunities for discursive and exploratory learning and high-level problem-solving and risk-taking.

4. Model high-level, subject-specific academic language

Setting up clear expectations for our students regarding linguistic precision

Our LAE students are like students everywhere in that they come to us fresh off the study of GCSEs that have become too narrow, too reductive and that don't seem to provide the language base that forms a robust basis for later study. They often arrive at the LAE hungry for learning but with a kind of linguistic tunnel vision. They can become locked onto ideas and often those are sincere and heartfelt, but they're also often just not very well-informed or well-expressed.

Students from more affluent homes, particularly those with professional parents, tend to deploy language with greater intent, as a tool for expressing precise thought, and show an acute sensitivity to exactly what the question is asking for. Less advantaged learners often have little experience of being asked to think within a discipline and may have been offered fewer opportunities to do so. *The way that we model and encourage precise language use in all courses is critical.* Make high-level academic and subject-specific language the norm. Excellence is a habit, we become what we consistently do, so focus throughout the course on establishing how to use language clearly. By appropriate use of academic and subject-specific language, the courses will encourage students to do the same. *Lower academic language skills often hold back more high-ability Disadvantaged students*, and we are sometimes guilty of undermining the significance and point of high-level, subject-specific language by dumbing down our own language to make it more 'accessible'. Make clear the level of language expected, as well as why: that language is there for a reason, and that is precision. A discipline's special language, illustrated using specialist terminology, acquires a meaning in one subject that can clash with more everyday usage. The students who confidently accept this have flair; they take risks. The way they choose and arrange words is nuanced. Their reference points are wider. Such confidence is often characterised by an understanding of the 'underlying game' of language, and vulnerable learners can remain defended, cautious, not wishing to let go of their customary way of expressing things. There is an all-too-understandable fear of rejection and failure. There are many vulnerable students who don't get to hear the vocabulary they need reinforced at home or in the playground. It is therefore vital that courses saturate students until this vocabulary is so second nature that learners can confidently move about within it. This in turn can help to minimise the danger of learners relying on spotting features, predictable responses and drilled analysis rather than a more instinctive, intuitive understanding of the language of the discipline.

5. Build in misconception tracking points and accredit previous learning

Clarifying what our students already know (or think that they know)

At the LAE we don't waste time on starters/fun lessons—but in a sharing of rigour. There is no time for slacking—we focus on high standards always.

It's the detailed knowledge that 'flavours the claim', so read together, unpick the literacy at the core and front load the difficulty. The pitch of a lesson needs to take our students to the very edge of what they think and know—and to keep them there.

Unless a course starts from where our students already are, it runs the risk of boring them senseless by repetition of already mastered knowledge and concepts. However, for some students, poor prior knowledge, together with the lack of rigour and knowledge required in some GCSE courses, or reliance on rote memorising, combine to form a weak foundation for progression to A-level learning. Quickly mapping what a student already knows, possibly using 'most difficult first' techniques, helps to highlight where the pinch points might be of any new learning they are embarking upon. *Set up the highest level of difficulty first. Ask the students how they would start with this. Why is it difficult? What strategies would help them? What should they do first? How would they justify their approach?* Take the students through well-annotated questioning approaches to a problem that offer a roadmap through, but not by giving solutions. In addition, correcting the misconceptions, confusions and misunderstandings from previous learning helps to provide a more solid foundation for future progression. So, examples from previous students highlighting where they went wrong and how they subsequently improved become key. The clarity also needs to be built in regarding subject-specific input from experts on how such misconceptions tend to arise and why these issues are inherently troublesome in a subject. The course itself needs to set up a pace that genuinely challenges the most able students and moves their learning on. But it also needs to be able to recognise when that pace should vary, and when students are fading. High-ability students also need pockets of time to consolidate and check their understanding—and as a result, they need courses that regularly have the inbuilt capacities to check that this is happening.

6. Establish a transformational course structure through a celebration of scholarship

Supporting our students who may struggle to believe in themselves

We are ordinary people like our students are, some of us just happen to have a Dr in front of our family name, which helps to make excellence normal—it becomes more feasible for our students. We bring our backgrounds with us into the LAE as an example that isn't just standard or mainstream. But we also explain the hard work and sacrifice that it takes too. Scholarship is always a bumpy ride.

There are numerous aspects to a student's home life and self-perception that can cause barriers to success. By immersing them in *an educational world that overtly values and celebrates academic learning* and assumes that the students are smart enough to cope, a course culture can infiltrate self-doubt, ensuring that they are reminded of the best they can be in every interaction. We can normalise and communicate academic excellence throughout the course by encouraging an intellectual curiosity and bravery that never sets academic learning as beyond anyone's reach. A celebration needs to be a regular feature of the course design, particularly at the times of the most challenging activities and tasks. Make the understanding that is gained explicit by encouraging students to reflect on and evaluate what they have managed to achieve. This helps to celebrate expertise and mastery and to normalise intellectual debate, specifically by talking about learning and studying as a reward in themselves. We need to promote their engagement with the unknown and away from steering their responses into 'right answer' tunnels. Having students confidently engage with diverse, highly challenging materials will itself help to *boost their notions of possibility*. The whole point of learners as 'experts in development' is that they need to grasp the essentials of a subject but also to understand how difficult and frustrating gaining scholarship can be for all students. The well-timed modelling of difficult concepts through short interventions, clear supportive messaging and *access to one-to-one interactions* when needed can help to shift self-belief. These students need to see themselves as high-achieving, doing well and wanting to do even better. Once a student sees that they can achieve excellence, it can be transformational. That student is never quite the same.

7. Ratchet up the difficulty in tasks to carefully build positive academic resilience

Ensuring our students see work and achievement as necessary for self-esteem, not vice versa

Resilience really isn't something abstract or even necessarily something inherent to the LAE student: resilience is built by carefully sequencing curriculum so that our students acquire more of the knowledge and skills necessary to do well in class and in assessments; the more they succeed, the more they are, generally, willing to take risks [with their learning]. But we also take risks, which they see. We're committed to treating [our students] more like undergraduates than typical A-level students. We provide extensive reading lists for each topic and we 'tier' those reading lists, so that they run from the very accessible to the very demanding.

Many students struggle to realise that the effect of achievement on self-concept is stronger than the effect of self-concept on achievement. Learning only really happens when we are subjected to cognitive strain, deliberately designed difficulty, as that is when we are required to fully concentrate. Strain is unpleasant and so we tend to avoid it, consciously or otherwise. Students need to grasp that there is no perfectly paved, easy road to success. It becomes less bumpy when students accept that they are supposed to think hard, pay attention and struggle. Praise, scaffolding and encouragement all too often replace rigour and challenge and may well have been heaped on them throughout their academic career in attempts to boost their self-esteem. By continually raising the bar for students, we can deliberately set up productive failure. Getting it wrong is progress, but only when students are forced into failure do they fully understand this. Students with uneven, spikier profiles often don't yet know the extent of what they don't know. They have not been exposed to their own ignorance as there is likely to have been little explicit interrogation by teachers of their views when they offer them. As a result, there can be a *significant fragility to the knowledge of such learners at the edges*. They need us only when they are in the gap – or liminal space – between knowing and not knowing something. We need to give students the time and encouragement to remain in liminal space for as long as is necessary, where they are more likely to make cognitive changes and master troubling new concepts rather than simply mimicking what they think we want them to say. An important element of any course is to ensure that *we don't inadvertently steal their struggle* from them, as the surest path to positive self-esteem is to succeed at something which they originally perceived would be extremely difficult. So, scaffolding their responses too overtly can have significant detrimental impact. They must learn to do hard things to feel good about themselves and we may short-circuit the opportunity for them to build self-confidence by accepting their second-best efforts or supporting them at each step towards an understanding. The best way to help students feel that they are succeeding is to help them to achieve that on their own. It does not matter if they struggle with these ideas, as that is a powerful motivation to continue engagement. Difficulty is part of the pleasure—the entertainment, the spur. It builds into the course design a focus on clear 'small win' interactions that boost confidence and help to smooth the way for the longer journey.

8. Teach to the top and go 'off piste'

Making explicit the indicators of excellence required by our students

We teach our students to expect regular opportunities to go far beyond the specification(s), so that they're grounded in the wider universe of our subject and not just the areas that they happen to cover for their

*A level. We're clear that there should be no spoon-feeding of under-
standing. Our students—whatever their background, whatever their
aptitude—are going to have to work hard to master this content and
they're going to know that the responsibility for understanding lies completely with them. Sometimes that means spending focused time with
our academic-in-residence on really advanced concepts, sometimes it
means access to university-level material.*

Until we make the high level, most challenging demands, we will never know
whether our students would have been capable of reaching the highest standards.
It is important to teach high-ability students beyond the exam requirements to
give them a wider perspective on a given subject. Simply following a curriculum
can be needlessly restrictive. Defining appropriate national levels of progress also
matter. It is essential to explore national versus local standards as *students from
more Disadvantaged backgrounds often believe that what happens in their school
is an indicator of what the national standards require.* Peer group influence has
a great impact on students and needs to be highlighted and deconstructed to
clearly assert to students what is required to achieve the top grades and to give
them a road map of how to get there. An effective course should explore what
features of a subject allow students to investigate and research, and thereby set
up issues and problems that experts in our subject face and deal with. It needs
to teach through deliberately and explicitly demanding questions and tasks, and
whenever possible to utilise real-world problems. It is important to ensure students
are routinely expected to give extended, reasoned answers and are at least given
the opportunity to have to support their viewpoint even in the face of criticism or
alternative viewpoints being offered. It is very powerful to trial research questions
and new technologies, when appropriate, and give the students the role of expert
in co-development in terms of the directions that can be taken.

9. Offer feedback and redrafting to increase student endeavours

Enabling our students to properly commit to an ethic of improvement

*One element with some of our more Disadvantaged students is that they
often don't realise that they aren't finishing off their arguments—they
don't make their points strongly enough, or respond well to counter-
argument, or feel the need to be specific. They need to 'hear' their
arguments out loud, which is why feedback and dialogue are key in
classrooms. Then they need to practise writing them down. They have to
understand academic persuasion.*

Courses need to incorporate an initial stage of self and peer review. This needs to contain suitably clear instruction on how to do this effectively and how to frame improvements. Students must get used to redrafting their own work after regular peer and then public critique sessions. *Ensure that all feedback is specific, directed work for the recipient.* In addition, unless we give them embedded and directed time in which they are required to act on any feedback that the course has given them, all that time may be wasted and will have little visible impact. We must plan time within schemes of work where students act on and consolidate the comments and feedback. Our students need an understanding of what an ethic of improvement looks like. Courses need to build in the messaging that *if submitted work isn't the best a student can do, then it isn't finished.* Any course needs to commit to training students on fair and honest feedback of others' work, suggesting that they use questions rather than statements to reduce any negative impact, that they depersonalise any commentary and add the phrase 'so that' onto any suggestions to explain why the change needs to happen, and to make explicit how the work will benefit. They will themselves learn nothing from our detailed commentary on their work unless it is at the very top end of what they can do. If it isn't, then they themselves, with a little thought, can easily make the required changes. Submitted work must not be seen as the end of the engagement; feedback offers them that sense of ownership and responsibility and re-engages them in the process of improvement. We should ensure that students extend their understanding by transforming information into different formats and requiring rewriting for different audiences in the tasks set. Actively get students to write their previous feedforward targets onto any new work. Students therefore have the deficit from the last piece of work visible in their mind when working on their new piece, so that they will not as easily forget or ignore feedback. By providing feedback only at the end of learning, students don't have an opportunity to act on it, so an online environment can be an ideal way to set up formative and diagnostic assessment.

10. Plan in complexity, debate and doubt

Encouraging confusion endurance with the security that our students also need

Not knowing is key, with LAE teachers not being seen as infallible experts, as if a teacher just knows everything, this can then lead to our students becoming passive. And intellectual humility matters even more, as teachers maintain a beginner's mind, predicated on a commitment to question what we think we know and believe. We set up interesting collisions between ideas, led by deep interest and uncertainty. We are travelling with them.

Puzzlement is a great way into an enquiry. Focus opening questions in the course by concentrating on phenomena that experts in the subject still cannot explain and examine why things are still uncertain. Design deliberate disorientation into the tasks to enable students to become defamiliarised so that they must then cope with and make sense of these experiences. Expose students to novel challenges that might deliberately threaten their self-esteem. Too many able students seem to think that effort is only for the inept, which can quickly lead to 'imposter syndrome', where a child never really believes that they are clever and thereby become far too reliant on externally given accreditation. Offer them the opportunity to make disparate connections and to apply existing knowledge to new challenges. Encourage students to consider and reflect on issues relevant to their subject to reach their own informed judgements. It is a useful angle *to make learning objectives broader by clustering them*. Highly able students can complete complex tasks which combine objectives. Additional challenge for these students can be added by applying the learning objectives in different or less familiar contexts. Another angle for increasing complexity is to *make learning objectives deeper* by increasing the levels of abstraction. This might be done by framing tasks which require the skills of analysis, synthesis and evaluation. Focus on content on the key issues, considered from different perspectives, providing students with a much-needed resource to enable them to start developing a deeper understanding of important issues for themselves.

Conclusion: Leadership takeaways for increasing challenge to achieve excellence

All of the above ideas can be summarised quite easily. The key element is about ensuring that teachers do not inadvertently *steal the struggle* from students. *What does this look like?* To start with, teachers need to feel comfortable when they set tasks that the activities are designed to provide and increase cognitive conflict, which may focus on exposing students to the often-contradictory dialogues within a discipline. It also means pitching lessons to both support and extend students, and ensuring scaffolding is removed in a timely manner. It involves not being squeamish about interrogating students to extend and justify their ideas, and requiring them to use high-level, subject-specific language in their responses. It also means teachers articulating the high expectations they have, promoting rigorous thinking by demonstrating and demanding it, and modelling and reinforcing scholarship by talking about what it looks like in their subject. Teachers must constantly check students' full understanding, while requiring them to do their absolute best work so that there is a normalising of the higher levels of effort the highest achievers are already committing to and so that feedback will be purposeful. Finally, it means developing and sharing a subject-specific understanding around the knowledge, skills and behaviours that truly distinguish top achievement.

References

Ofsted (2013) *The Most Able Students: Are They Doing as well as They Should in Our Non-selective Secondary Schools?* London: Ofsted. Available at: www.gov.uk/government/publications/are-the-most-able-students-doing-as-well-as-they-should-in-our-secondary-schools (accessed 23/07/2023).

Ofsted (2015) *The Most Able Students: An Update on Progress since June 2013.* London: Ofsted. Available at: www.gov.uk/government/publications/the-most-able-students-an-update-on-progress-since-june-2013 (accessed 23/07/2023).

5
How Do We Ensure that Teaching is Always as Good as It Can Be?

High-quality professional development, professional development that responds to teachers' needs and stays relevant to the classroom experience, is one of the key ways leadership [in any school] can demonstrate that they genuinely value teachers as professionals. It's not about a search for 'silver bullets', or rigidly applying the latest conference or article takeaway without considering the subject or class context: it's about searching for, and reaching, a point of collective agreement on features that underpin great teaching.

LAE Assistant Head

This book makes the case for a distinct pedagogy that addresses the needs and aspirations of academically high-attaining students. We argue that how these students should be taught is often different from how we teach students who achieve in other ways. And we argue that there is a national priority to do so.

We think that is a profound claim, enough for one book, and perhaps a career or two, but it is a limited claim. We do *not* say that other, more generalist pedagogies are irrelevant to teaching academically able students. We do not argue against the validity of quality-first teaching, or 'getting it right first time'. We do not launch a vigorous polemic in support of academic attainment at the expense of other types of attainment, still less in support of academic selection in all schools. Nonetheless, we believe that the success of the LAE is at least *prima facie* evidence that academically able students flourish when they receive a particular type of education involving a particular type of teaching.

This chapter is about how the LAE leadership ensures that students receive that type of teaching. In the words of one far-sighted former Assistant Head: '*Top end subject knowledge is the key requirement [for teaching at the LAE]. The pitch of each lesson needs to take students to the very edge of what they think and know—and to keep them there.*' We're dealing here with the nuts and bolts of school life. Much of what follows is about the systems, processes and artefacts the LAE uses continually to improve the quality of teaching and learning through our continuous professional development (CPD) programme. We should say at the outset that none of this—*none* of it—is as important as the *culture of scholarship* that needs to permeate every interaction, between teachers, between teachers and students, and between students. Equally important is the observation that there is no magic here, only serious thinking and hard work. The LAE works as well as it does because its leadership and teaching faculty have spent the time to fashion its artefacts and to precision-engineer its systems. That process has not always involved invention but it *has* involved a great deal of critical thinking about what works best most often. As scholars—that word again—we believe that everything we do should be built on solid evidence as interpreted by those with relevant expertise. But professional opinion cannot be taken on trust or adopted without first developing a deep understanding of how any system or strategy will function in our context. In other words, yes, we've stolen and we've emulated a lot, but we've thought carefully about who we've stolen from, what we've emulated, and how both would help enrich our students' lives and learning. We have also come up with some of our own ideas.

Teaching and learning at LAE

In a practical sense, the lodestars for great teaching at the LAE are the school's Learning Essentials. We'll turn to those shortly. The Learning Essentials are described as follows in the school's *Teaching and Learning Handbook*:

> The LEA Learning Essentials provide a framework for teachers to
> support students from all backgrounds to access the most demanding,

most rewarding degree and degree-equivalent courses and to progress to the most demanding, most rewarding professions. We want to develop academically resilient learners who are fully prepared to lead happy, productive adult lives and to contribute positively to society.

The above is deliberately consonant with our statement of curriculum intent—so that, in Counsell's terms, the *how* of what of we do (pedagogy) is always oriented towards and evaluated in terms of the *what* of what we do (curriculum content) (Counsell, 2016). There is a clear focus on Disadvantage ('students from all backgrounds') and a setting of expectations of progress, attainment and destinations ('most demanding, most rewarding degree and degree-equivalent courses and … professions'). There is also a clear focus on wellbeing and citizenship. The point is not to virtue signal, although we think there are many virtues contained in the paragraph above. The point is to set expectations that learning in our school is about *all* of the above. Quite apart from being an exam factory or academic hothouse, both labels that have mistakenly been applied to LAE, the school prides itself on the holistic nature of the education it provides.

LEA teaching is characterised by:

AGENCY   Teachers seek and achieve impact on their students' learning, their colleagues' development and the school's overall effectiveness.

INNOVATION   Teachers are encouraged to trial, evaluate, share and adopt new ideas and strategies based on the best available evidence.

RIGOUR   Teachers have the highest expectations of themselves and their students.

For several years, the first of these characteristics was another 'A', for Autonomy. Successive surveys demonstrate that teachers value autonomy. One of the most recent, by the National Foundation for Educational Research (NFER) and the Teacher Development Trust, concludes that 'teacher autonomy is strongly correlated with job satisfaction, perceptions of workload manageability and intention to stay in the profession' (Worth and Van den Brande, 2020). This all sounds very affirmative. And we are certainly not arguing for ever greater central direction—whether from the senior leadership team, the multi-academy trust, local authority or from central government. But we have at least three reasons for preferring agency as a cardinal virtue. As a rallying cry for teachers, 'autonomy' carries risks.

First, the desire for autonomy is all too often based on the false precept that other professionals enjoy greater autonomy and less accountability than do teachers. Teachers without substantial experience of other professions (the clear majority) can hardly help but reflect on the routines that characterise a day in the life of even the most liberal school, not to mention the sheer tonnage of bureaucracy that characterises our education system, and long for a little autonomy. Indeed, that is precisely the sentiment captured in the NFER report. Teachers, it concludes, have lower levels of autonomy than doctors, engineers, lawyers, nurses, etc. Taking the argument one step further, the lower levels of autonomy experienced by teachers help explain the higher rates of burn-out, and turnover more generally, among teachers than among those in other professions. But this is not quite right, or at least it is not the whole picture. The research on which the NFER draws, from the UK Household Longitudinal Survey (UKHLS), actually measures *self-reported* autonomy, or, put another way, *perceived* autonomy. Perceived autonomy is a useful way of comparing professions that have little else in common, from professional practice to an institutional setting to degree of official oversight, etc. It is, in fact, easier to measure perceived autonomy than actual autonomy, but we must understand them as different.

Crucially, perceived autonomy depends in large part on expectations. How much autonomy did you *expect* to have when you became a teacher or when you took up your current post? Teaching is one of the few professions in which impressions of professional practice can date from childhood. It is also one of the rare professions in which the central activity, the thing new entrants want to do most, is experienced almost immediately and with very limited supervision. We can hardly imagine doctors consulting with patients without live supervision after only a few weeks of classroom preparation, but this is exactly how early career teachers learn their craft. Both are reasons to suspect that teachers may have higher expectations of autonomy on entering the profession than is typical in other fields. It certainly seems a more plausible explanation for the survey results than actual differences in systems and processes across sectors. Can we really conclude that a nurse working in a busy, successful hospital is subject to any less rigid a set of routines than a teacher in a busy, successful school? Do we really believe that a solicitor's regular supervision sessions, a legal requirement of their continued ability to practise law, bear a lower standard of accountability than a teacher meeting with their head of department? These assumptions seem, at the very least, questionable. None of this is a reason for complacency about high levels of dissatisfaction among teachers, but it does suggest a different potential remedy—namely, a more informed and realistic dialogue about the profession, its opportunities and its pressures, relative to other professions. The belief not only that teachers should be autonomous but that other professionals actually *are* autonomous, risks contributing to the cognitive dissonance that drives colleagues out of the teaching profession.

The second risk inherent in fostering an attachment to autonomy, is that it frustrates, or at least exerts tension on, attempts to cultivate collaboration. Teaching is a necessarily collaborative activity. For all that we motivate aspiring and early career teachers with notions of individual impact and one-to-one relationships with students, the evidence overwhelmingly supports the conclusion that students achieve better when the average quality of teaching rises, rather than when they have an individually brilliant teacher (King, 2003). This can seem less intuitive in an academic sixth form context than in a primary or secondary school where subject expertise is less obviously to the forefront of teachers' ability to achieve impact. But a moment's reflection on the importance of factors such as the culture of scholarship (see Chapter 6) and the (relatively consistent) behaviours for learning that support high academic achievement in different fields, should make it clear that the importance of average teacher quality is undiminished.

Finally, prioritising individual autonomy does not sit well with the search for best practice, or the obligation, firmly established in the medical profession, to identify and use the most effective known methods when addressing the needs of those in our care. Organisations like the Education Endowment Foundation have established a beachhead of evidence-informed practice in schools through its popular *Teaching and Learning Toolkit* and its network of Research Schools. In the past few years, Ofsted has adopted a more consistently evidence-informed approach to key topics such as curriculum development while sensibly shying away from previous diktats about pedagogy based on less thorough evidence. In the independent sectors, forward thinking schools such as Eton College have established centres for teaching and learning with the explicit mandate to promote and contribute to the emerging national and international consensus about those elements of teaching practice that work best within subjects and across subjects. Set against these valuable initiatives, the celebration of autonomy looks rather like an excuse to opt out of proven teaching strategies.

Agency, on the other hand, has none of these drawbacks. There is a rich discussion of agency in the social sciences that has been applied to teachers by sociologists of education. Agency can be thought of in straightforward terms as the 'capacity to act' and in slightly more involved terms as 'active efforts to make choices and intentional action in way *that makes a significant difference*' (Toom et al., 2015: 615, original italics/italics added). Toom et al. are particularly good on teacher agency and are worth quoting at length. Teachers, they observe:

> …engage in innovative thinking, adapt themselves to diverse requirements in their working environment, interpret and negotiate with both their colleagues and with parents the multiple possibilities implied by policies, make independent choices and find a balance between their personal preferences and shared collegiate understandings … [to build] a relevant, inspiring and constructive environment for their pupils and themselves and their colleagues. (Toom et al., 2015: 615)

Priestley et al. argue that teachers' agency is achieved through the complex interplay of school context, school systems and individual expertise and personality traits (Priestley et al., 2015). At the LAE, that means that teachers are actively involved not only in their own professional development, but also in the continuous improvement of the school as a whole. In the words of the LAE's long-serving lead teacher of physics: '*When I first started teaching [here], I was drawn to autonomy because I was happy with the idea that I could teach how I wanted as long as I achieved the results the school expected of me. I've come around to the idea that [that] was quite narrow-minded of me and it's maybe more affiliative, more reflective of the responsibility I owe to my colleagues, to consider what I can learn and what I can contribute to making all of our practice better.*'

Agency, it should be noted, *assumes* high degrees of professional trust. Teachers are unlikely to experiment and to take sensible risks with learning—recall that the second of the key LAE principles is innovation—if they feel they will suffer professionally every time that experimentation goes wrong. And go wrong it will. Even enthusiastic amateur athletes, actors and musicians know that peak performance often involves operating at the edge of competence in order, eventually, to extend competence. The jazz pianist Herbie Hancock is fond of telling audiences about an early interaction with Miles Davis, shortly after he joined Miles' second greater quartet in the early 1960s. After a respectable but staid club performance, Hancock apologised to his band leader for having not played more creatively over a new piece. 'I haven't practised it enough', Hancock said. Davis is said to have replied without hesitation: 'I pay you to practise on the bandstand'.[1] One of the things that we like about this anecdote is that it completely circumvents the false dichotomy that too often prevails in schools between trust and accountability. There is no sense in which Davis, a famously temperamental character and brutal taskmaster, was indicating that he would accept a poor performance in front of paying customers—he was also quite mercurial—but he understood, intuitively, that creative practice involves risk and that performers needed the freedom to take risk as well as the judgement to know which risks to take and which to avoid.

Professional trust is often equated with respect, which consistently ranks as one of the most important drivers of satisfaction in the workplace. When teachers talk about professional trust, they are typically referring to two things: being trusted to choose the teaching strategies they employ most often in the classroom and being trusted to set, or at least significantly to drive, the

---

1   Quoted in full, Davis's response includes plenty of epithets that fall well outside our definition of scholarly language. The culture of the bandstand and the culture of the school are, in some respects, quite different.

professional development goals for which they will be held accountable. At the LAE, professional development opportunities change throughout the year. During the first school term, they are set at the whole-school level, based on evidence collected through lesson observations, learning walks, analysis of students' achievement and their work, and what students tell us about their learning experiences in and outside the classroom. These inset sessions can be considered 'top down', in that they establish common priorities for all teachers, but great care is taken to adapt the training provided both for different subject areas and for teachers' differing aptitudes and degrees of skill. As the school year progresses and more evidence is gathered, colleagues are encouraged to work in more bespoke ways as part of professional learning communities. Some of these communities continue to work directly on priorities established at the beginning of the year, although not necessarily in the ways originally envisioned. Some groups' priorities change in response to changes in students' achievement. And some groups pursue research agendas of their own devising. As the school's Assistant Head for Research in Learning says: '*The personal interests of teachers really matter and need to be facilitated through a CPD programme that enables them to properly identify an informed focus and what they want/need to work on.*' Coordinating all this activity and preserving throughout the potential for all colleagues to learn from the work of others requires not just careful planning and keen logistics, but also a well-crafted language for learning that binds together everything we do. That function is served by the LAE Learning Essentials.

The LAE Learning Essentials

The LAE Learning Essentials document LAE teachers' 'collective agreement', referred to at the start of this chapter, about those features that underpin great teaching and learning (see Table 5.1).

There is no great originality in having such a list. Most effective schools will have their own and, in practice, for obvious reasons, there will be substantial overlap between them. Why should the LAE favour these criteria, in particular? The Learning Essentials are a self-conscious attempt to chart a course between the Ofsted framework that applies to all schools in England and Wales and the Teaching Excellence Framework used in British universities (The Schools Inspection Handbook, 2019). Both sets of standards seem important reference points for an academic sixth form school. The LAE's teachers need to align their practice with a national understanding of what works best in most schools most of the time, while also understanding the expectations to which their students will shortly be subject on the most

Table 5.1: The LAE Learning Essentials

1.	Teachers and students exemplify the LAE's **Core Values**–Excellence, Independence, Resilience, Respect, Humility and Kindness–in their behaviours and relationships in and outside the classroom.
2.	Teachers **model** expertise through exceptional subject knowledge, clear instruction, engaging explanations and examples, and sophisticated questioning.
3.	Students' learning is **sequenced** cumulatively to build knowledge and understanding, including by 'front loading' the most challenging content; through regular, planned retrieval practice; and by signposting links between current, prior and future learning.
4.	Teachers **adapt** instruction and provide personalised **feedback** based on regular, accurate **assessment** of students' understanding; anticipating common misconceptions wherever possible.
5.	Students are consistently challenged to **think hard** about the most transformative ideas in their chosen subjects and to develop understanding beyond the specification and into undergraduate study.
6.	Every opportunity is taken to prepare students for life in **modern Britain**, for further study and for professional working life.
7.	Teachers and students **speak** and **write** clearly using Standard English, using vocabulary appropriate to subject domain, social context and intent.
8.	Teachers and students make effective and responsible use of learning technologies, including generative **artificial intelligence**, to enhance access to the curriculum and nurture the adaptability needed for future landscapes..

demanding degree courses at the best British universities. (There is a parallel set of expectations for the growing number of students who pursue degree-level apprenticeships.) The drafting of a set of Learning Essentials involves compromise. In the latest iteration of the Learning Essentials, the school leadership felt it necessary to employ Ofsted's preferred term 'adaptation' rather than 'responsiveness', not because of any profound semiotic difference between the terms, but because all schools need to speak the language of their principal regulator. The Learning Essentials also draw heavily on academic research into effective teaching and learning. Again, as an academic school, our teachers have a healthy respect for the evidence base underpinning standards of understanding in their subject areas; they bring the same respect for evidence to bear on their understanding of pedagogy.

Why stop at eight 'essentials'? A longer list is always possible, although much longer and it starts to trigger uncomfortable memories of lesson observation criteria of old—faintly ridiculous tick lists containing dozens of supposedly observable practices. On the other hand, a shorter list is hard to imagine without giving up something that is, well, essential. There is a healthy dollop of pragmatism applied in their drafting. From experience, eight standards are at the upper limit of standardised success criteria than can be practically applied to an activity as varied as teaching and learning. The Learning Essentials are a work-in-progress; they always will be. This is a strength, not a weakness.

As educators, we should always be willing regularly to revisit the Learning Essentials in light of an evolving evidence base and changing priorities. The latest iteration of the Learning Essentials was introduced in the 2022–23 school year and placed greater emphasis than previous iterations on formative assessment, adaptive teaching and personalised feedback. These were not areas of weakness, but they were areas where we felt that additional valuable work had been done by teacher educators and where we felt our own evidence suggested our shared practice could be stronger.

Still, it's worth highlighting a few features of the Learning Essentials that are particularly important in context. First, we speak of Learning Essentials, not Lesson Essentials. If the terms 'learning' and 'lesson' are coterminous, something has gone very badly wrong—particularly at our phase of education. Lessons should be seen as interventions—or, perhaps, 'nodal points', if that helps avoid the baggage associated with the word 'intervention' in UK schools— in the learning process. Effective lessons accelerate learning. Highly effective teaching, in and outside lessons, accelerates learning more. But a great deal of success at our phase of education depends directly on learning that is more curated than taught, and sometimes, crucially, is entirely independent of professional guidance. What Biesta called the 'fragile interplay between the teacher and the student' in respect of learning is better conceived at our stage of education as a progressive passing of the torch (Biesta, 2012: 42).

At the risk of sounding hackneyed, our values really do matter. Placing them at the top of the list signals very clearly that outstanding learning happens in an environment characterised by respect and humility, and where both students and teachers feel both valued and empowered. According to a long-serving lead teacher: '*Every staff and student survey demonstrates [that] … both teachers and students feel they can really contribute to the school, its success, its risk taking. Combined, these are the bases for success.*'

The most ambitious of the Learning Essentials is the expectation that students think hard about the most transformative ideas in their chosen subjects and develop understanding equivalent to that typically acquired during undergraduate study. As Headteacher, one of Alex's most consistent creative challenges to the LAE faculty is to make the first year of university boring. This is a tongue-in-cheek way of reframing expectations of curriculum content and student achievement. Why shouldn't curious, industrious and confident students who will shortly attend Cambridge, the LSE (London School of Economics) or UCL (University College London) engage seriously with the ideas they will encounter at those universities a few months early? Why should certain journal articles, books or field studies be considered *de rigueur* in September but impossibly intimidating the preceding January? Why should the idea of higher learning be regarded as putting more foundational learning at risk, as opposed to underscoring the importance of that learning?

An excellent example can be taken from the LAE's economics department. The school's lead teacher of economics provides students with an expansive reading list, tiered according to difficulty. The most basic materials are found in any school resource plan: textbooks authorised by the exam board, articles from *Economics Today* and the *Financial Times*. These serve the needs of the curriculum narrowly defined. But the rest of the list includes articles from journals such as *The Economic Journal*, the *American Economic Review* and *The Journal of Political Economy*. The reading list is scaffolded according to the topics that occur within the A-level syllabus, those that branch off it and those that are wholly outside its remit. Some of the articles relate to content with which students would not typically be expected to engage until they are studying for their Master's degrees. *'The point'*, he says, *'is to normalise challenge, to get [the students] used to engaging with more challenging ideas and to know that it's okay not to understand everything the first, second or even the third time of reading. Sometimes you crib one idea from a journal article that you're otherwise completely stumped by, but that one idea is more important than the magazine article you scanned in 30 seconds and understood completely.'* This sort of ambitious approach to learning requires resilience from the student but also humility from the teacher. *'The most challenging material also provides a meeting place with your students. I'm not claiming that, in every case, I will understand the most advanced concepts better than the students do. But that's okay.'*

The obligation to evidence

Professor Dylan Wiliam, one of the most important educational voices of the past 25 years, has spoken persuasively about the classroom as a 'wicked' learning environment. He argues that the nature of learning as a process and the classroom as an environment conspire to make third-party evaluation of teacher impact treacherous and self-evaluation all but impossible. 'The difficulty', he argues 'is [that] we look at the teacher, and we see the results, and we assume it is the teacher causing those results'. *Post hoc ergo propter hoc*. In fact, both teachers and their observers tend to mistake students' performance in the short term—in the very short term, if we are considering 20-minute lesson observations—for learning that *by definition* happens over the long term. Almost all schools in England operated a regimen of 'high stakes', or graded, lesson observations for part of their history. The LAE almost certainly retained this practice for too long. The approach the school takes today is informed by changing national and international understanding of the pitfalls of lesson observations and focuses less on summary judgements about teacher quality and more on the search for reliable evidence of learning.

This approach requires middle and senior leaders—generally, but not exclusively, those who observe lessons—to consider pedagogy in the subject context, to admit that the most effective strategies for teaching hyperbolic functions may bear only superficial comparison to those best suited to teaching, say, the dramatic function of catharsis or Schmitt's state of exception to the principle of sovereignty. This is not to invalidate consideration of classroom practices such as questioning, adaptation or the ratio of direct instruction to deliberate practice, but it is to dissuade the observer from assuming that those practices are governed by a universal logic rather than one linked directly to context. The LAE's prevailing model of lesson observation also understands the lesson, or section of a lesson, as one input into a broader evaluation of the learning experience. This requires observers to consider factors such as curriculum planning and sequencing, students' recall of previously taught topics, students' assessed work and their folders of notes, as having equal weight in the overall assessment of the quality of learning.

Lesson observations are nodal points in an ongoing quality assurance process. A typical lesson observation will focus on one of the LAE Learning Essentials, the selection of which reflecting either whole school, departmental or teacher priorities depending on the point in the year. The observed teacher will know in advance the focus on the observation. They will also know that observers are looking for evidence of routine practice rather than anything 'showy' or theatrical. By contrast, experimentation *is* encouraged and can be signalled in advance to the benefit of both parties. Observers do not ignore evidence of other Learning Essentials, but the identification of a clear, mutually understood focus helps both in the quest for overall consistency and in the marshalling of robust relevant evidence. Lesson observations provide an opportunity for a professional dialogue about students' progress. That dialogue should be timely. The school requires post-observation dialogue to take place within 24 hours of the observation itself. Observers are encouraged to start that dialogue by listing dispassionately the evidence they gathered during their observation, rather than by inviting the observed teacher to reflect on the effectiveness of their practice. This is more a matter of methodological integrity than a matter of respect, although the one implies the other. One indication of colleagues' investment in developing their practice is found in the value they attach to these dialogues. The LAE calendar offers ample opportunities for learning walks and other low-stakes to no-stakes observations. The school's policy is that these practices do not need to be followed-up with a formal conversation. The policy is honoured more in the breach than the observance because teachers typically *request* feedback or *want* to talk about their practice.

Recruiting for subject expertise

First Who, Then What—or, 'get the right people on the bus, then figure out where to go'—is an idea popularised by the management theorist Jim Collins in his book *Good to Great* (2001), and has subsequently been so widely cited as to have surrendered to cliché. School leaders often baulk at Collins' nostrum, when it is quoted at them. With serial under-recruitment of teachers, particularly in maths and sciences, regional disparities in teacher supply and high rates of turnover among qualified teachers, Headteachers can all too often feel as if getting anyone on the bus is nigh impossible.

The LAE does not have any magic lure for recruiting teachers. Some of its terms and conditions are favourable. Sixth form schools typically have slightly shorter terms and slightly longer summer holidays than primary or secondary schools. The degree of passive supervision required for students aged 16–19 is less than for those who are younger, and the range of extraordinary duties required of teachers is correspondingly lower. Managing student behaviour—it must be admitted—is nothing like the challenge that it can be in more comprehensive environments where most students will be younger than 16. On the other hand, the school pays the same as other schools in inner London. The school day is longer than most secondary schools, with timetabled activity from 8:25 am until 5 pm most days, and large numbers of students are on site both before and after those times. Inevitably, given the nature of the A-level curriculum, marking students work is a significant source of workload.

What the LAE does have is a clear sense of what it is looking for and the culture it is trying to preserve and enrich. LAE teachers are subject experts first and foremost. This is not to say they don't require other qualities or that there aren't many fine people in many fine schools who see themselves quite differently. But for a school with the LAE's ethos, subject expertise is non-negotiable. Michael Young memorably framed the difference between university lecturers and secondary school teachers in terms of vocation—the former expand the field of specialist knowledge through research and the latter disseminate existing specialist knowledge through teaching— rather than in terms of their relative depth of expertise (Young, 2014). That spirit informs the LAE approach to teacher recruitment. Expertise is often indicated by formal qualifications. All LAE teachers require at least a good first degree in the subject they will teach or in a closely related field. Three quarters of the school's teaching staff have Master's degrees. Unlike many schools, those Master's degrees tend to be subject related rather than linked to an aspect of teaching practice. One third of LAE teachers have PhDs, including those colleagues who have joined the school through its academic-in-residence programme. But certification is at best an imperfect proxy for expertise or enthusiasm. Many people drift rather than dive into Master's degrees, or even PhDs, and, in any case, having once been very interested in a specific area of research is no guarantee that you will remain so 10 or 15 years into a teaching career. By contrast, some colleagues who have progressed straight from a first degree into teaching or another profession retain a lifelong passion for study in their chosen field.

The recruitment process must therefore find solid evidence both of relevant subject expertise and of the sort of infectious enthusiasm necessary to stimulate that interest in students. The LAE requires an academic interview for all teaching posts. This interview, one of three, is as important as the candidate's lesson observation or interview with the Headteacher. During the academic interview, lead teachers and senior leaders with relevant expertise ask searching questions about subject domain, curriculum design and subject-specific pedagogy. These interviews are always recorded and scored according to agreed success criteria. The interviews always follow broadly the same structure as a competitive university interview, starting with expected knowledge and understanding (the specification), venturing into sought-after knowledge and understanding (the subject domain), and concluding with mental agility in the face of uncertainty.

As experienced interviewers will know, the most obvious questions are often the questions that candidates struggle to answer. Teachers are always asked to describe what great teaching and learning in their subject 'looks like'. Given what we've written elsewhere in this book, it's clear that we think there's a wrong answer to this question. The wrong answer goes something like this: 'Great teaching is great teaching. Full stop. [Insert subject] teaching is no different.' This far-from-hypothetical answer fails on all counts. Either the candidate has decided that the most generic aspects of their practice are the only aspects that significantly affect students' learning, or they do not recognise the features of their subject that make it a coherent and distinct focus of ongoing academic (or professional) research. If that thought isn't immediately concerning, flip the answer around and imagine telling an A-level student that the most important thing they were doing in their psychology lesson were learning the rules of an information hunt or how to mind map.

There are as many right answers to the great teaching question as there are subjects taught in our schools and colleges. The following examples, taken from transcripts of interviews with successful candidates, give a flavour of what a 'right' answer, in our terms, sounds like. In the first case, a high-performing history teacher explains what she would expect from a history lesson:

> Great history teaching involves a deep sense of enquiry, of students engaging with the evidence of past events, wherever possible through access to primary sources, and with how those events have been interpreted by historians and subsequent generations. In a great history lesson, classroom conversations will involve challenge to both evidence and interpretation: How do we know this happened that way? Is the evidence fully convincing on this point? Does this or that interpretation really seem convincing based on what we know already? A great history scheme of work will involve the progressive accumulation of knowledge but also of what can be considered knowledge and what is interpretation.

There's a certain resonance with this next example, given by an economics teacher:

> Great economics [teaching] involves engaging with real-world problems. Students will know the textbook because they have to [for examination purposes], but they'll also interact directly with real data sets. … If I were

> trying to explain the PSBR [public sector borrowing requirement], I'd want
> to go first to the ONS [Office for National Statistics] website and then to
> the way organisations like the IFS [Institute for Fiscal Studies] interpret
> those figures. It's inevitable that students [who haven't encountered these
> ideas before] will see them as somewhat abstract, but they also have to
> understand that they're very real.
>
> What these examples have in common is the fusion of the what and the how. What
> is being taught determines how it should best be taught. There are, of course, simi-
> larities in strategies, and these similarities increase as the subject domains grow
> closer, but the teachers themselves conceive these strategies (and execute them)
> in entirely subject-specific terms. This is entirely aligned to the school's learning
> essentials. They also have one more thing in common: a focus on the reality of
> what is being taught. Despite the term 'academic' often being used pejoratively
> to denote abstract or cloistered, the LAE teaching faculty finds it to be anything
> but. The subjects we teach are tools to understand and to change the world, not
> refuges from it. This also reflects the character of the teaching faculty. More LAE
> teachers—again, around a third—have substantial experience in another career
> than would typically be the case in the maintained sector.

Conclusion: Leadership takeaways for developing the curriculum

English education policy for at least the past decade has focused on governance—
or who does and does not get to run schools—and on curriculum—or what
young people should learn. The central questions of *who* should be teaching
in schools and *how* they should teach has attracted perplexingly less attention.
We believe that this is a serious mistake and that the national conversation
should reorient back towards a sustained discussion about teachers' professional development. As it relates to the core concern of this book—the education of academically high-attaining students from economically less advantaged
backgrounds—teachers' professional development should focus on the con-
joined accumulation of subject and pedagogical expertise rather than succumb
to any false choice between them. Young people will not, as a rule, acquire
academic expertise unless they are surrounded by adults who can model it,
inspire it and structure learning so that expertise can be acquired and retained.
This effort will require a rethinking of the currently rather sharply drawn distinctions between national expectations of what great teaching looks like in
colleges and universities and what it looks like in schools. It will also require
constructive dialogue between the independent sector, which has taken full
advantage of the lower level of social challenge it faces to sustain its focus on

academic achievement, and the maintained sector, which has cultivated deep expertise in adaptation to meet the needs of a wider cross-section of the population. In the first decade of its existence, the LAE has proven a liminal creature, tucked away in a narrow crease between higher education, independent and maintained schooling. Its success suggests that this is a richer seam to mine than many more mainstream stakeholders may have appreciated. The time has surely come for this experience to be shared more widely.

References

Biesta, G. J. J. (2012) Giving teaching back to education: responding to the disappearance of the teacher. *Phenomenology & Practice*, 6(2), 35–49.

Collins, J. (2001) *Good to Great: Why Some Companies Make the Leap… and Others Don't*. New York: Random House.

Counsell, C. (2016) Genericism's children. *The Dignity of the Thing* [Blog]. Available at: https://thedignityofthethingblog.wordpress.com/2016/01/11/genericisms-children/ (accessed 23/07/2023).

King, K. (2003) *Keeping Pace with Technology: Educational Technology that Transforms. Vol. 2: The Challenge and Promise for Higher Education Faculty*. Cresskill, NJ: Hampton Press.

Priestley, M., Biesta, G. J. J., and Robinson, S. (2015) Teacher agency: what is it and why does it matter? In R. Kneyber and J. Evers (eds.), *Flip the System: Changing Education from the Bottom Up*. Abingdon, UK: Routledge.

Toom, A., Pyhältö, K., and Rust, F. O. C. (2015) Teachers' professional agency in contradictory times. *Teachers and Teaching*, 21(6), 615–623.

Worth, J., and Van den Brande, J. (2020) *Teacher Autonomy: How Does It Relate to Job Satisfaction and Retention?* Slough: National Foundation for Educational Research/Teacher Development Trust. Available at: www.nfer.ac.uk/media/3874/teacher_autonomy_how_does_it_relate_to_job_satisfaction_and_retention.pdf (accessed 23/07/2023).

6
Making Scholars Feel Safe and Supported

In October 2022, the LAE was privileged to find itself in the top three schools worldwide, in the Supporting Healthy Lives category of the T4 World's Best School Prizes. This category recognises schools that provide access, relevance and opportunities for students, staff and the community to develop healthy habits, behaviours, knowledge and skills. The school was judged on the understanding that health is about balance, resiliency and consistency, and has many components, including mental, physical, nutrition, personal safety, environment and emotional health. The selection was based on whether a school or college was judged to be implementing world-class strategies in a planned, integrated and holistic and sustainable way.

Some may have found the LAE's prominence in this category surprising. The school has a very strong academic track record, which many educators unfairly believe to be somehow incompatible with supporting 'healthy lives'. In fact, high attainment is often mistaken as a signifier that a school must be an 'exam factory', a ruthless machine for churning out grades rather than people and which leaves students battling imposter syndrome if not mental burnout.

Core to the LAE model is the opposite belief: that young people can only thrive academically if they are thriving personally. The school's prioritisation of safety and wellbeing are, therefore, at the very heart of its success.

The strength of the LAE is in its people and the distributed leadership across the school—staff *and* students. We know that this is because of the 'LAE family' ethos, which permeates throughout the school and in turn influences leaders when making any new staff appointment to the school. In this chapter, we will be investigating what pastoral support, personal development and wellbeing look like at the LAE, and how this might be spread more widely across the school system.

What underpins the academic success?

The LAE is a wonderfully vibrant and diverse community of scholars in a densely urban setting characterised by significant deprivation, challenge, ambition and aspiration. The school community welcomes 500 students and over 70 staff to a safe and inclusive school environment each day. For many students, LAE is a place of safety unlike any other available to them. Students undergoing significant personal challenge routinely tell their teachers that they want to come into school because it is the place they feel most safe and supported. Leaders set, model and exemplify very high expectations of how the whole school community should work together to achieve collective and individual success. This begins in very small ways. Notwithstanding the age of the students, the Head and senior leaders insist on greeting them at the school entrance each morning and sending them home at the end of a long school day. Across the school, there is a clear and palpable love of learning demonstrated by all, and a desire to promote mastery of learning concepts and content. In a recent review, the quality of 'relational safeguarding' at the LAE, a measure of how connected students and staff feel to one another and how this supports their sense of security, was described by inspectors from the London Borough of Newham as 'exceptional' and 'unlike anything previously experienced [in schools]' (London Borough of Newham, January 2023).

Safeguarding is genuinely at the core of everything we do. We invest a great deal of time, effort, thought and evidence-informed practice into culture, learning and human behaviours that are required to get the best from students and staff. Safeguarding is everyone's business, and the effectiveness of any school, leadership, relationship and achievement is predicated on the principles of safeguarding, with middle and senior leaders working together with student leaders to conduct their own 'deep dives' into institutional safeguarding, so as to enrich their knowledge and understanding, while also heightening their awareness of the significantly positive impact of human relations in safeguarding practices.

Relational safeguarding and student voice

There is no one strategy that can encapsulate all safeguarding practice. In the following pages we will describe some, though not all, of the systems and processes the LAE uses to keep its students safe. But if there is one *principle* that sits at the core of the LAE approach to safeguarding it is to invest in relationships with students and between students, to remain in dialogue with them and to take their feedback seriously at all levels of the school. It has become fashionable to refer to this principle as *relational safeguarding*. With regards to raising an issue of concern in school or about school, students are involved in courageous reporting. This system allows students to report issues anonymously if necessary. The students insist that the reporting results in change and that complaints are not ignored. The impact of effective relational safeguarding on students' wellbeing is palpable. LAE conducts regular surveys to promote a culture of safety regarding issues such as bullying and delivers regular information evenings to parents on how to keep their children safe. Survey results consistently show very high positive response rates for all pastoral and safeguarding questions. In the last student survey, 95% of students reported that they '*feel safe in school*'.

An important piece of work conducted during the first half of 2023 illustrates the importance both of relational safeguarding and of courageous reporting. The school's Deputy Head identified that female students did better in subjects and classes where they were in the majority and less well in those where they were in the minority. The Senior Leadership Team conducted structured interviews with groups of female students to take their feedback and better to understand their experiences. The group was then invited to present to the school's Education Committee. The young women that presented to the Committee felt that their male counterparts seemed more confident and their contributions to class discussion seemed to be taken more seriously in what one described as the 'clever subjects' (i.e., physics and further maths). One of the female students had dropped further maths and one had dropped physics, despite feeling that their teachers had made considerable efforts to persuade them to change their minds. Female students felt that the problem comes, in part, from the feeder schools, which include single-sex schools. The female students spoke of a strong female maths teacher who had helped to change their perception of maths as a 'male' subject. The findings of the interviews led directly to training for teachers in those subjects aimed at increasing the amount of female learners' voice in classroom discussions.

Embedded leadership of safeguarding across the school

A genuinely safe school requires investment in people at all levels. The Safeguarding Governor is the serving headteacher of one of the LAE's partner schools, a recognised expert in safeguarding and a highly experienced school governor in both the state and independent sectors. The Safeguarding Governor described the school's strengths as a 'determination to go above and beyond, being nurturing, caring and values driven'. The Safeguarding Governor visits the LAE every term, actively reviewing records, the Single Central Record, and checking action points recorded and progress on them, in individual cases. He also chairs a Safeguarding Committee, the purpose of which is not only to scrutinise safeguarding practice at the LAE, but also to investigate emerging trends and to research best practice across London and nationally. The Safeguarding Committee routinely meets with students to investigate their experience of life at the school. An annual safeguarding report is presented to the Safeguarding Governor, who is of the opinion that the Designated Safeguarding Lead (DSL) and the pastoral welfare team are highly effective in responding to any safeguarding or student issues and challenges, and in identifying trends of behaviour and risks. They are clear and assertive in making recommendations for improvements to policy, practices and routines, and in not holding back on making any necessary changes as required to further refine and strengthen safeguarding practices across the school in line with local arrangements and national legislative requirements as set by the Department for Education.

Senior and middle leaders model through their own behaviours, actions, tone and practice that safeguarding is their highest priority. Through their supervision, training and development, they routinely record, track, monitor and report on safeguarding incidents by type, nature, level of seriousness and in relation to the more sophisticated use of trend and student-level analysis of behaviours, the management of incidents as reported and observed, and the engagement of students in their learning and development, such as their attendance and participation levels in both formal and informal curriculum. The Head and Deputy Head routinely attend the weekly safeguarding review meeting and the Heads of the school's six Houses have recently undergone training to become deputy designated safeguarding leads, extending further the qualified support network.

Senior leaders approach matters relating to staff conduct and discipline by promoting effective interactions and strong relationships, and in upholding professional standards in a way that is supportive rather than eliciting a punitive response. For example, the response leaders took to students who were found vaping is an educational learning response, and this includes involving parents in supporting their learning about it and supporting the school.

Restorative, therapeutic, evidence-informed and strengths-based in approach, this means that any matter relating to conduct, whether of staff or students, will be treated respectfully, humanely, and with care and consideration always upholding the school's ethos.

An important factor has been the creation of a culture of vigilance, where our learners' welfare is actively promoted. Students are listened to closely and this is monitored through termly surveys, a student council and auditing by the Senior Leadership Team and Safeguarding Governor. Staff are trained to identify when a student may be at risk of neglect, abuse or exploitation, and they report their concerns. Leaders and staff work effectively with external partners to support students who are at risk or who are the subject of a multi-agency plan.

Leaders at all levels are aware of their safeguarding duties and responsibilities. There is a very high level of investment in staff training and development around all safeguarding protocols and practices, particularly when making referrals to middle and senior leaders where there are concerns about a student's safety and wellbeing. There are well-established and embedded protocols and practices in place for all to follow, supported by a pastoral support team, including a qualified SENCO and a Pastoral Manager. Safeguarding training, as required by *Keeping Children Safe in Education* (Department for Education, 2023), has been arranged for all governors and all staff are adequately trained, as highlighted in their recruitment and development records. As a school that highly values formative assessment, there are dedicated safeguarding questions for interview candidates and regular safeguarding quizzes for staff.

There is a specialist counselling service in place for any student or staff member. The school doubled its counselling provision in response to the spike in anxiety and mental ill health following the onset of the Covid 19 pandemic. Students report that they feel very well cared for, supported and nurtured in their day-to-day interactions with staff. Similarly, staff report that they feel valued, respected, cared for, nurtured and supported to achieve their goals and to be the best they can be for their students and in pursuing their career goals.

As with most schools, a robust Prevent risk assessment has been put together, in liaison with the local authority Prevent officer, to ensure that students are protected from radicalisation. A log of all incidents is kept and reviewed regularly to spot any trends and patterns. All staff receive the latest Prevent training and it is part of the induction of new staff. All members of the Senior Leadership Team (SLT) have completed safer recruitment training.

Our House and tutor system, alongside the Safeguarding team, have built a professional and supportive culture throughout the school. The safeguarding team monitor and review all cases where there are unusual risk factors affecting a student's safety or wellbeing. They meet regularly with the students involved, liaising actively with the internal and external stakeholders that must work together to keep the student safe. Safeguarding is rigorous and effective, and students feel safe because they know that all staff will act on any concerns.

Vertical tutoring

LAE students are grouped into vertical tutor groups including students in Year 12 and Year 13. This provides a vital opportunity for relationship building, for sharing culture and for addressing the sorts of debilitating anxieties that are all too common at this stage of education. One of these is imposter syndrome. It is hardly surprising that some students, when thrust into an environment known for high achievement, may experience some nervousness about whether they 'deserve' their place at the school. This is particularly true in a setting such as the LAE which typically draws from over 100 secondary schools per year. Students new to the LAE are often accustomed to being academically at the top of any class in which they find themselves. That can't remain true for everyone. Formal and informal mentorship from older students is incredibly effective at building resilience in new students and helping them to hold onto and grow their sense of self worth. The vertical tutorial system also allows older students to pass on their accumulated learning from the first year of their A level studies and to serve as role models for how to handle the inevitable pressure of university applications and preparations for public examinations. One student commented that the vertical tutoring system was important because '*We all come from different cultures in our secondary schools and we need to be able to be happy in this school and to understand how it works.*' The principle of vertical tutoring has proven so effective, in fact, that many of the school's larger departments organise virtual 'summits' with 'Year 14' students, those who have recently graduated and are studying at university. Learning from those students' successes, and minor failures, is among the most valuable opportunities available to LAE students.

Student networks and ambassadors

Students who are listened to and who develop strong, trusted relationships with one another can quickly be empowered to take a prominent role in the life of the school. One of the most distinctive but least recognised features of life at the LAE is the operation of its exceptional student networks. Recognised student networks co-lead many aspects of school life and contribute to ensuring that the school is a vibrant, engaging and fun place for their peers to be, as well as running many of the most influential initiatives across the college. Students who are part of the formal leadership groupings and pathways offered to them, whether in the form of the School Council or the network groups, are exemplary role models to their peers, not only because of the high level of interpersonal and intra-personal communication skills they routinely demonstrate, but also in the resilience and determination they show in driving their individual and collective leadership agenda on behalf of the student body.

The student-led Mental Health Network

As an example, there is a student-led Mental Health Network (MHN), which is the longest running network across the school and provides learners with many benefits in such an academically rigorous institution. The network organises a full day of learning every year to reduce the stigma that may be associated with mental health issues and to encourage students to speak freely about their own experiences of managing and supporting mental health crisis. The network organises an assembly each half-term to cover issues such as the effect of social media on mental health, the importance of positive body image, or neurodiversity. Recently, the group has done important work highlighting the pressures on mental wellbeing among male students. They add wellbeing tips into the student bulletin. Students are very clear about wanting to be able to raise these concerns with ease and to talk about the posters in the student toilets that give details about reporting issues. They mentioned a 'chain of command' of wellbeing ambassadors, form tutors and the safeguarding team. Following the Covid-19 pandemic, there has been a greater understanding of the impact that having a mental health network in the school environment can have on the students and teachers, and how important it is to ensure that everyone feels as though they are part of a community.

The network is set up in a way that allows the students themselves to be the fundamental catalysts for change in the school community. In their own words: *'The shared vision of the MHN is to challenge the stigma surrounding conversations of mental health and create a more supportive environment between students and teachers. It is our belief that all students should be supported for positive mental health and the network helps to identify and respond to barriers that may exist, to make this happen. To implement this idea into the network the students send out weekly wellbeing tips in our school's newsletter. This includes tips on activities or habits that students can adopt into their daily lives to improve general health and wellbeing. We have also created a monthly teacher toolkit, where learners provide a student lens on their experience at school that they share with all teachers. This may include things such as what it is like to feel imposter syndrome or to live with a mental health illness.'*

Given that this is a student-led network, the voices of those involved are absolutely critical to understanding what this series of interventions looks like, what impact it has, as well as what it means for the students who take responsibility for running the activities across the college. In the video that supported the World's Best School bid, one student commented that through this network:

We create an environment of support for the students as they understand that we are in the same position as them and so can relate to their problems and struggles which we too might have experienced. Through this we can give the best advice on situations, some advice which teachers or senior members of staff may not be able to give. As well as creating a safe environment for the students, we also help the teachers as we provide the teachers with appreciation throughout the year to thank them for the support and effort they put in day in and day out. We also believe that our work to break down the stigma surrounding mental health should include the wider community as well as LAE. The network has helped me develop further as a person through the way in which it has allowed me to express empathy and compassion. And allowed me to bring about education on topics pertaining to mental health which I feel aren't spoken about enough. We understand that a good mental health is at the forefront of everything we do in our lives so understand that by educating ourselves on mental health we can live better lives.

Another student, offered insights into some of the specific mechanisms that the Mental Health Network uses to bring about this student vision, including the annual personal development day, where the students take responsibility for creating a series of workshops, trips, activities and visiting speakers on the theme of mental health that all students attend:

We create a menu of activities, many of which we run ourselves, that students then select their preferences for. We as students come up with the ideas ourselves and run workshops that include both active examples of wellbeing activities (such as mindfulness and journalling) as well as educational spaces where students can understand better the complexities of adolescent mental health from experts. We run campaigns across the year raising awareness on mental health and will speak regularly in our weekly school assemblies as a space to educate the student body. For example, with men's mental health we try to deconstruct the stigma surrounding men's mental health specifically and have taught students how to tell if your friend may be silently suffering.

People may be suffering despite seeming fine and okay and it's impor-
tant to provide a safe space. We also educated about neurodiversity
and what it is. How it affects mental health as 'atypical' people may feel
excluded and isolated from society. This allowed a friend of mine to feel
safe speaking about his ADHD and how it makes him
feel. … Another important annual event for us is appreciation day.
This is a day where we create a number of different ways that we can
all appreciate classmates, friends and teachers by writing messages
and preparing gift hampers for individual teachers that are specifically
personalised. We had a message wall set up in the common room and
personal letters people could gift to each other writing custom messages
to their friends. I feel a great sense of pride and responsibility in my role
as a leader of the Mental Health Network. I think it is important that all
schools have student leaders that are given a platform to advocate for
mental health and are also empowered to be change-makers within the
school for creating a culture of kindness and support.

Another student serves as a wellbeing ambassador. A network of these ambassadors runs in parallel with the Mental Health Network in the sense that they
are student leaders who are working to enhance the mental health and wellbeing of the students in the school. They work alongside school staff to develop
new approaches to support students' wellbeing and mental health. They are
selected each year through a rigorous application process and begin their programme with an intense training module on adolescent mental health. Their
training continues through studying the practices that an online platform called
Selfology provides with regard to issues such as meditation and rumination.
All ambassadors are given free access to this programme, where they look at
current research and understanding and become informed as to the current
trends and challenges.

One wellbeing ambassador (WBA) sheds light on the significance of her
role and, incidentally, on how seriously she takes this responsibility. She states:

As ambassadors it is vital that we are aware of strategies to monitor
and take care of our own wellbeing. We complete thorough training
about how to approach discussion around and dealing with wellbeing
issues. For example, it was made very clear about the importance of
being non-judgemental and empathetic. Therefore, when I first started
the role, we engaged in in-depth research into the mental health of
the current students by running a wellbeing survey and conducting
focus groups with a range of different students. Once we analysed the
responses, we narrowed down the most prominent issues that came up.
Naturally, with our school being a very academic school, stress about

grades and learning was expectedly at the top of the list. … Arising out
of this research, we then ideate on a series of different interventions that
we feel would have the most impact on a school level. From here a little
bit of problem solving was required when brainstorming what possible
solutions could be implemented … we grouped all the ideas into high
maintenance, low maintenance, small impact and large impact. After
much debate and democratic voting, we narrowed down our plans to
two initiatives. We create a proposal of these initiatives that we present
to the school's senior leadership team. Examples of projects in previous
years have included peer mentoring and bespoke school planners that
contain detailed wellbeing advice and sample CBT [cognitive behav-
ioural therapy] worksheets. One year the WBAs redesigned the school's
academic mentoring programme to include wellbeing questions that all
Tutors were discussing with their Tutees on a regular basis, in addi-
tion to questions about academic progress. At the end of the interven-
tion, we evaluate the impact of the project and recommend whether the
intervention should continue in future years. This cycle then contin-
ues again in the next academic year with a new cohort of WBAs that
ensures that there is a culture of continually improving the wellbeing
provision within the school through a research-based methodology. So
far, I have gained valuable awareness and sensitivity to other people,
particularly my college peers. The skills I am learning now, I believe,
will be crucial in my future ventures, whatever they may be.

The student networks take their nurturing and educational role very seriously.
One student said: '*We're like big brothers and sisters. We've been through it; we*
know what it's like and how they feel.' Year 13 student leaders are acutely aware
that they need to train the Year 12 students to take over the leadership of these
networks before they became consumed with work for their final exams.

The LAE personal development curriculum

Although the LAE is one of the highest-performing academic sixth forms in
the United Kingdom, the school is about much more than grades. An intellectually exciting curriculum encourages a love of scholarship and a sense
of wonderment about the world in learners. Students study hard, but also
throw themselves into a rich and rewarding co-curricular programme, including sport, music and the performing arts, and opportunities to volunteer with
local charities and social enterprises and other forms of civic engagement. This
broad-based education allows students to explore their interests, develop their

character and refine their talents. A key aspect here is that the students challenge each other to achieve more than they might alone, but also encourage and support each other along the way.

An alphabetical list from 2022–23 serves to illustrate the breadth of interests in the student body. There are an Amnesty youth group, art club, astrophysics club, baking club, BAME network, bioart: dissecting and drawing club, book club: gods, goddesses, mortals and monsters, chess club, circus club, cool choir, creative writing club, debate club, excel club, eco network, global affairs club, go club, guitar club, historical film club, Japanese club, karaoke club, LAE news, maths club, mental harmony club, music appreciation club, nature club, origami club, personal growth and development, philosophy society, political discussion, practical chemistry club, psychology society, poker club, and even a scrabble club.

Diving into just a few examples of the personal development curriculum (PDC) serves to highlight that it is not simply the breadth that impresses so much as how seriously students regard the care and support that they offer to each other. In one student's own words:

The focus of the Mental Harmony club is on improved concentration and mental clarity. Explore the concept of emotional intelligence and the ability to relate to others and oneself with kindness, acceptance and compassion. Some of the activities and questions explored during the sessions will include: meditation; acts of kindness; what makes us happy; challenging negative schemas; judging life positively and feeling good.

Students speak highly of the cooperation between the different student networks (e.g., the BAME Network, LGBTQ+ Network and Gender Equality Network, ECO, etc.). Indeed, the work of the students has extended beyond the school itself. The LGBTQ+ group is heavily involved in the Stratford Youth Centre. The individual networks have focus groups too. The network leaders receive special lanyards, are well known within the school and have a high profile in assemblies. The school was awarded the Gold category in the Leeds Beckett LGBTQ+ Inclusion in Education Award. The student-led equality groups have supported the school's equality message through assemblies, charity events and campaigns. They have also been successful in connecting with the local community, with the BAME network supporting a Newham Council campaign championing BAME students' voices, the LGBT+ Network being actively involved in the recruitment of a local LGBT+ youth worker and the Gender Equality Network representing the school at a consortium of school feminist societies. Issues explored by the networks included discrimination and micro-aggression. The BAME network ran cultural exchange sessions for Black History Month. Students also ran a session on Islamophobia.

The students are proud to have created groups that did not exist in their 11–16 school provision. One female student said that she felt that LGBTQ+ students had a high status in the school, something that she had not experienced in her 11–16 education.

Another student-led Personal Growth and Development club is based on the premise that

> *we can all do with some time to check in on ourselves, step off the hamster wheel and think creatively about how to change our experience for the better. It is about starting to shed self-limiting thought patterns in order to be authentic to yourself. It will be a structured mix of journaling, mindfulness, relaxation and creative exercises, and designed to be laid back and fun. You do not have to share what you discover in the process unless you wish to do so: there will be some respectful pair-work talking but no massive show and tells in front of a group of people.*

School assemblies

School assemblies are co-planned and co-delivered with students; they feature relatively little of the sermonising that characterises routine assemblies in many, if not most, schools. Assemblies always begin with a performance by a student. Often this is a musical performance by one of LAE's many accomplished musicians, but it can also include spoken poetry, examples of visual artwork or a reading. A senior teacher or member of the school leadership will then present on a theme for the week before handing over the bulk of the time on stage to students from the School Council or one of the Networks to present on a topic they find stimulating or important. One recent assembly explored dialects and how they alter and define us as individuals. This topic was treated sensitively, emphasising the value of students' own voices and dialect as part of their unique identity and cultural reference.

A school assembly was a way of introducing a mental health worker to the students, who were encouraged to approach her on Mondays with their issues and suggestions. At another assembly, the ECO network group spoke about the 'Just Stop Oil' protests. This was a brave topic to address and the students weighed the place of activism in a democratic society versus the cost of disruption to many people's daily routines. It was followed by an excellent presentation about an Amnesty International campaign and a wonderful talk from a student about the exhibition that she was mounting in the Horniman Museum about her North African culture. Throughout the assembly, the school's core values were exemplified.

The co-curricular programme

Co-curricular and super-curricular programmes are offered to students by LAE staff and partners. They provide students with higher levels of access and an opportunity to engage in academia and commerce. An extensive programme of extra- and super-curricular learning is provided to all students, drawing on the wealth of sporting, arts, music and performance venues found locally, and indeed nationally. LAE students make extensive use of the community of Newham and the immediate surroundings to extend their access to high-quality learning, sporting and performance venues, as well as to local and international businesses which are now locating into the former Olympic site at Stratford. Students benefit from a timetabled sporting afternoon on Wednesdays, and on Thursday afternoon they can participate in the clubs or networks they have elected. The importance of demonstrating social responsibility individually and collectively is made very clear to students and staff by school leaders, in part as a response to the school mission for social mobility. Multiple, extensive and carefully selected school partnerships provide students and staff with the very best learning and growth opportunities to become successful, but they are also encouraged to seek out new opportunities which can only further strengthen the curriculum on offer to the school community, both locally and internationally. Compulsory sport and weekly self-improvement, as well as following interests, such as music and drama, have been demonstrated to be helpful to students in building their self-esteem and confidence.

The school contracts professional personal education organisations to deliver sex and relationships education during the academic year, and the students have appreciated this element of their PSHE in their feedback about these sessions.

School counselling team

The intensity of the academic regime in the school has led to a 'transition list' meeting every week for pastoral staff, who identify individual students of particular concern. Early Help provision planning in school has doubled in the number of referrals made to the externally appointed school counselling team. The school counsellor supports students with study, personal and family issues, which includes anxiety, depression, anger management, perfectionism, sexual identity, sleeping and eating problems, post-traumatic stress disorder (PTSD), domestic abuse, self-harm and bereavement. The counselling team provides a report annually for the DSL. The service is also offered to staff.

Staff used the House point system, which is aligned to the core values of the school, to praise students and were active in ensuring that all students attended electives. Students report that they find pastoral sessions supportive and they recognise the extensive efforts made by their tutors and support staff to give them the very best chances of success during their time at the school.

The School Council

The School Council plays an active role in exemplifying the school vision, values and ethos, as does the pastoral 'House' system and the numerous charity events and activities that take place. Students engage intellectually with controversial and contemporary issues through the lecture programme, PSHE tutorials and the large number of educational trips and visits that take place.

It is recognised by the students that the Senior Leadership Team implements much of what is suggested by the School Council, and they support the students in implementing the changes that they seek. The School Council meets to vote on new initiatives. The student leaders have access to the termly and yearly student questionnaires. They meet with governors (including the Safeguarding Governor) and feel that their voice is taken seriously. The School Council is aware of historical matters relating to equalities raised on the matter of a communal reflection/prayer facility, as requested by former and current students. Although the school previously provided such facilities at a nearby community centre, representatives of the student body expressed their desire for an onsite prayer facility, as a matter of priority and urgency, to prevent them using their valuable lunch time to walk to and from the facility, pray, and still have time to eat their lunch. This resulted in the school recently re-introducing a discrete multi-faith prayer facility onsite, and is testament to the collaborative ways in which the school and student leadership teams work together for the benefit of the entire school community.

Scholars' programme

One subtle but important way in which schools can contribute to students' wellbeing is by choosing what and who to reward and to recognise. LAE scholarships are awarded on the same progressive basis as school admissions. First, weighting is given to contextual factors included in the school's Index of Need; then, students are ranked according to academic achievement. The result is a scholars group made up of the highest attaining students but also those who are making the most progress in their studies. As the gap between identifiable groups narrows over the course of Year 12, scholarships align more naturally with absolute achievement, although the progressive weighting is never entirely abandoned. In addition to the whole school scholarships, the LAE also offers maths, economics and modern languages scholarships, which come with a financial reward but, more importantly, university trips, lectures, books, calculators, mentoring and subsidised overseas work experience. One recent student said that the opportunity to visit Oxford University as part of the scholars' programme really helped him to stay focused on what he was aiming for. Sure enough, the student achieved three A*s and is now studying engineering at Oxford.

Safeguarding Culture and Practice Review

Where is the 'hard' evidence that any of this works in the way we claim? In 2022-23, the governors and Headteacher commissioned a new service provided by the London Borough of Newham (the school's Local Authority) which reviews the safeguarding culture and practices found in a school based on 'lived experiences', as reported by students and staff and observed during the review process. The LAE commissioned this new service to explore the extent to which the policy, practices and procedures, as set by governors and leaders, contribute to the educational effectiveness and performance of the school as well as the outcomes achieved by students. Leaders were particularly keen to engage with officers of the Local Authority (LA) in providing a constructive and evidence-based review of the safeguarding culture and practices found in the school since it is now more than ten years since the school first opened in 2012. The LA officers were invited to cast a critical eye over our safeguarding procedures, to establish if we had any institutional blindspots. They selected three 'lenses of enquiry'. These were:

Relational Safeguarding - the extent to which interrelational and intra-relational communications between members of the school community, staff, students and governors promotes a strong culture of safety, harmony, equality and respect, and how this impacts on the wellbeing and achievement of all in the school whether this be during formal learning times, informal break or lunch periods, the start and end of a school day, or the way in which students and staff co-exist and work together to achieve their collective success.

Environmental Safeguarding - the extent to which the internal and external, including online, environment promotes a culture of safety, safeguarding, wellbeing, dignity, respect and community cohesion. This includes a review of policies, procedures, practices and daily routines, as well as a look at the facilities made available to provide a holistic education and enrichment experience.

Leadership of Safeguarding - the extent to which leaders and governors, including student leaders, promote, embed and secure a culture of safety, wellbeing, harmony, equality, dignity and respect, so that every member of the school community is respected and valued, and in doing so can achieve their goals to be successful.

After several days of extensive interviews with students, staff, the Senior Leadership Team and governors, the Newham team came to the following conclusion:

> In summary, the LAE is an exceptional place where all members of the school community are kept safe, very well supported personally, academically and professionally to achieve great success and to thrive within the LAE 'family' ethos, where leaders and governors have high aspirations and ambitions for everyone. … It is the view of the review team that the leadership of LAE, as demonstrated by all leaders, is exceptional. It is the view of the local authority, following their visit to the school, that the leaders and governors can confidently raise their bar further beyond reaching excellence to being exceptional in all that the school community can achieve. This is a testament to the dedication, loyalty, commitment and servitude given by leaders across the school, including the student leadership team, to ensure LAE provides every member of the school community a place where they can truly thrive; indeed, they do! This is quite remarkable an accolade to give, but truly deserved.

The LAE is fortunate enough to have received many accolades. None is more important than the conclusion above.

Conclusion and leadership takeaways

LAE Governors have set a very clear mission and vision to provide a high-quality education underpinned by the desire to increase the social mobility of those students who are most Disadvantaged in and outside Newham, and who are academically able, across the 16–19 age range. This vision is sustained and in the tenth year of operation. The school is quite literally providing life-changing opportunities for significant numbers of Disadvantaged young people to learn. It is a place where any student or staff member, no matter their unique characteristics or individual needs, can truly thrive and be successful in cultivating their goals, ambitions and careers within a family ethos of support, challenge, nurture and aspiration for all. The ambition is clear for everyone to aspire, succeed and to be excellent, if not exceptional, in all that they do and become. The values set by the Governors and leaders—Excellence, Humility, Independence, Kindness, Resilience and Respect—genuinely permeate throughout the entire school and the people who work and learn there each day in their thoughts, words and actions.

References

Department for Education (DfE) (2023) *Keeping Children Safe in Education 2023: Statutory Guidance for Schools and Colleges*. London: DfE. Available at: https://assets.publishing.service.gov.uk/government/uploads/system/uploads/attachment_data/file/1161273/Keeping_children_safe_in_education_2023_-_statutory_guidance_for_schools_and_colleges.pdf (accessed 23/07/2023).

London Borough of Newham (2022) *LAE Safeguarding Culture and Practice Review*. London: The London Academy of Excellence (28–29 November).

7
Greater Expectations: Student Destinations

The LAE is fortunate in having a growing international reputation. Several times a year, the school is visited by delegates from other parts of the world— ministers, civil servants, school district administrators—typically, those with national or regional responsibility for school systems. During a recent visit, the Minister of Education of a Gulf State gave a candid assessment of what effective schooling means: 'I'm interested in where your students *go* [when they leave you]. What schools [universities] do they attend? What jobs do they have five and ten years into their career?' As educators, we are bound to point out that there is a great deal missing from this definition—the quality of the student experience and the positive development of their character, for example—but there is no denying its clarity. As a North Star metric, student destinations *are* a good proxy for school effectiveness. They are better than exam results, certainly, and particularly if your school mission is centrally concerned with advancing students' social mobility. Fortunately, LAE students have progressed in large numbers to prestigious universities. The first few graduating cohorts are now young people in their mid-20s, many of whom are doctors, lawyers, entrepreneurs, financiers, politicians and technologists. The credit for these achievements belongs most directly to these young people themselves. But it would not have been possible without the extensive investment the school has made in creating dedicated time and staffing to prepare students properly for their future universities and careers. We fully understand that both these factors—compulsory, time-tabled lessons or seminars focusing on life beyond school and the staff quali-fied to run those sessions—are more easily marshalled in a sixth form school than in a secondary school with multiple competing demands on resourcing. The invidious decision whether to deploy your qualified physics teacher—assuming you have one—to prepare Year 12 students for careers in engineer-ing or to teach catch-up maths to students in Year 9 is not one that we face. Nonetheless, we hope that there are lessons to be learned from our very particular experience. This chapter has no pretension to be comprehensive; instead, it will focus on those features of LAE provision that seem most dis-tinctive in the maintained schools landscape.

University preparation

The LAE is probably best known as one of a handful of state schools chal-lenging the historic stranglehold that fee-paying independent schools have enjoyed on admission to Britain's most prestigious universities. That reputa-tion is a mixed blessing. The profile it brings has helped the LAE further its core mission in many ways, not least through the convening power it con-fers and the access to stakeholders who have come to support our careers programme (see below). But, in all candour, the LAE's leaders and gover-nors would rather its reputation rested on broader measures of contextual achievement. The fact that a state school, for example, sends dozens of stu-dents to Cambridge each year may be exceptional, but it is less significant than the fact that those students come from families and districts with little to no prior access to higher education or that they have spent time in care. Similarly, the public focus on admissions to Oxford and Cambridge is not entirely healthy, however much it serves as a sort of national shorthand for social mobility. The LAE is no less proud of the students it sends to a host of universities, or, increasingly, to degree-level apprenticeships, than it is of those who proceed to the two universities that garner most attention. Still, for a certain audience and readership, what interest the LAE holds depends heavily on its track record at securing places for its students at better-known universities and medical schools. To pose directly the question that both authors are most frequently asked (less directly) at conferences and Teach Meets: How do we do it?

Challenging truths

Let's begin with two challenging truths about university preparation. First, there is no discrete programme designed to prepare young people for this or that university that matters anything like as much as the nature of the education they receive every day. Of course, Oxbridge and medical school candidates at the LAE receive specific attention and training in the process of applying to those universities. We will expand on that preparation below, but mostly it consists of following advice freely available from the universities themselves. The distinguishing feature of successful Oxbridge candidates, at the LAE as elsewhere, is the authenticity of their scholarship, which, at age 17, has far more to do with how candidates *apply* what they know, with how they think, than with the extensiveness of what they know. The fact that so many teachers and school leaders believe otherwise is partly a function of the status quo, in which most schools never send enough candidates to either university to develop genuine expertise in the admissions process, and partly a function of the *de facto* pedagogical model that has crept into our many schools: that of teaching to the test.

The second challenging truth about university preparation is that staffing matters. The people best placed to prepare young people for the process of applying to a selective university are generally people who have been successful in securing a place at that university for themselves. This is not the same as saying that all graduates of that university give quality advice on applications, and there are exceptions to this, as to all, rules. Nonetheless, in much the same way as most professional football managers tend to have been professional players, most successful Oxbridge coordinators tend to be Oxbridge graduates. This is not because Oxbridge graduates *sui generis* have some more profound claim to scholarship than others—we do not. It is because there are nuances to any admissions process best learned through personal experience. The situation is slightly different regarding medical school admissions only because there are rather fewer qualified doctors pursuing second careers in teaching.

Normalise the university experience

With those qualifications to the fore, there are, of course, practical steps that schools can take to prepare all students, but particularly those who are socio-economically Disadvantaged, for the process of applying to highly competitive universities. The first of these is to normalise the university experience. Some of this is a matter of environment and social convention. Students attending schools dating from the fifteenth or sixteenth centuries, which are arranged around one or more quad, boast a chapel, practise formal dining, at which teachers wear academic robes, either periodically or as a matter of course. Such students will find most Oxbridge colleges all too familiar. Students who have grown up in urban environments and attended schools with none of those characteristics face something of an adjustment. In the case of many LAE students, there is the additional psychological hurdle of having grown up in one of, if not *the* most ethnically diverse environments in the UK and being asked to relocate to towns and cities far more reflective of the country's overall demographic. The following can stand as a fairly typical reflection on the part of a Year 12 LAE student: *'There's a part of me that's just so drawn to the idea of studying there [at Oxford] but there's also a part of me that just can't* see *myself there.'* There is a great deal to unpack and to address in that statement, but the most immediate priority is that students should have the opportunity to visit Oxford or Cambridge as part of a programme of university trips in Year 12. Oxford and Cambridge colleges vary in their willingness to host school parties at different points in the year, but students can gain a great deal simply from wandering around either city and imagining themselves studying there. This does not have to be seen as an attempt at persuasion. A student who gazes up at the Bridge of Sighs and realises that this is simply not for her may have made exactly the right decision; at the very least, it will be a more informed decision than is possible without the visit. Schools will reach different decisions regarding whether a whole cohort trip to Oxford or Cambridge is appropriate. For the LAE, it makes sense to take all students to one or another of those universities as early as possible in Year 12, if only to begin to combat the risk of imposter syndrome or other factors proving a bar to applications from students from less advantaged homes.

The second practical step schools can take to normalise the university experience is to cultivate students' capacity for independent learning. In Chapter 5 on developing teaching, we explain that the LAE Learning Essentials were in part informed by the *Teaching Excellence Framework* used in higher education (Office for Students, Published 24 June 2020 Last updated 28 September 2023). There remains a basic tension in our education system between what is recognised as effective pedagogy in secondary and further education versus what is recognised in higher education. Whether these differences are a necessary consequence of differences in student population, age range or content being taught, or whether they reflect how each phase of education is staffed and regulated, is an intriguing topic but outside the scope of this chapter. The fact is that state-educated students too often reach university accustomed to a diet of rigid classroom organisation, high-velocity learning activities, routine formative assessment and individualised feedback and extensive opportunities for intervention, or catch-up, only to find themselves required to make onward academic progress based on pedagogical input that requires vastly greater independence and engagement with learning opportunities of a totally different type. Schools can progressively introduce this style of learning throughout the sixth form phase, not as a replacement for more conventional secondary pedagogy, but as a supplement to it. The weekly LAE lecture programme, for example, is a vital opportunity for students to learn how to sustain their engagement without the routine opportunities for deliberate practice common in a classroom. They are taught to listen actively, to take notes, to screen for relevance, to summarise, to plan questions and, in the case of guest lecturers, to value learning even in the absence of an ongoing relationship with their 'teacher'. These are all vital sources of academic resilience that students will need to be successful in applying for and attending more competitive universities.

Establish more tailored provision

Turning to more tailored provision for applicants, LAE students applying for more competitive university courses—including, but not limited to, Oxford and Cambridge—take part in masterclasses organised by subject teachers. The expectation for these masterclasses is that they go meaningfully beyond the examination specification, both in terms of subject content covered and the sophistication with which it is covered. For example, the A-level politics specification includes a taxonomy of actors in the international system that reflects academic work of the late 1990s and political reality of the early 1990s. The specification recognises states and a variety of 'non-state' actors that can be sorted into various camps, such as transnational corporations, international institutions, inter-governmental organisations, etc. The specification offers neither scope nor explicit reward for exploring an inherently problematic organisation (both morally and intellectually), such as the Wagner Group, which is simultaneously a private sector actor, a sometime instrument of Russian foreign policy, a tool of Russian President Vladimir Putin's personal power, and a competitor to the Russian military. Equally pertinent, the A-level chemistry specification requires students to understand the half-life equation and to apply it to experimental data. But Oxbridge chemists should be able to derive the equation from first principles, thinking carefully about what the numerical measure of a rate of reaction actually *is*, and solving some differential equations. The integral calculus involved is less a stumbling block than identifying the correct differential equation to apply and using the chemistry to figure out what limits to put on the integrals. These are exactly the sort of 'troublesome' topics that might come up in the famed 'second movement' of a university interview and should be explored in a masterclass unconstrained by the limitations of the exam specification.

Identifying the right course

Finally, there are the more routine aspects of preparing students for the application process itself. This requires dedicated staffing and time. The LAE has a dedicated Oxbridge Coordinator who receives an additional allowance and a reduction in timetabled hours for the role. The school timetable includes an hour for explicit university preparation and students are expected to conduct significant independent research in their own time. Students should be encouraged to research thoroughly the range of courses available to them rather than to apply to the course that is nominally closest to their favourite A level or A-level module. The breadth of courses available at Oxford and Cambridge alone is exceptional and merits sustained exploration. The ratio of applicants to available places is a consideration here. Students should no more be herded towards an inappropriate choice of course than they should be towards an inappropriate choice of university. But a young person needs to know if they are competing against nine other candidates or against 40 and prepare themselves accordingly. At the LAE, students are always strongly encouraged to identify the right course first and the college or university second. Specific aptitude tests linked to course choice are common and students will need to be prepared for these exams in the same way as they would any other external assessment. This need not be as extensive as the preparation for A levels, but students should expect to be prepared for the structure of the assessment, the form of questions it will contain, and should expect to sit one or two practice papers and to receive detailed feedback on their performance. Finally, the interview process—much mythologised—requires preparation. Students should expect to undergo practice interviews with people who have attended the university to which they are applying. As a practical matter, these interviewers may not all be drawn from the teaching faculty. There are positive benefits to applicants undergoing at least one interview with an unfamiliar interviewer as this will help prepare for a key psychological pressure point. Establishing connections with local employers is often a good route to identifying graduates who can stand in as interviewers. The LAE is also at a stage in its maturity where alumni are increasingly important to preparing current students for applications to more competitive universities. This can be by providing specific feedback on their experience as applicants, by helping with more advanced subject contact or simply by being on-hand as a local point of contact when students attend in-person interviews. We appreciate that this is an example of success breeding success. Not all schools will be in this position. But more progressive Oxford and Cambridge colleges offer similar support networks of their own and groups of schools might work together to produce something similar.

Careers education

School-based careers programmes too often confront a basic mismatch between responsibility and expertise. For eminently practical reasons, careers advice and guidance in schools is typically delivered by people with little or no direct experience of working outside the education sector. Consoling assumptions that teachers are professionals like any other, and therefore well placed to deliver guidance regarding the mores and expectations of working in other sectors, ignore the idiosyncrasy both of schools and of teaching relative to the broader economy. In fact, there is growing evidence to suggest that teachers' understanding of the labour market is quite limited, even when it comes to their own employment prospects in adjacent sectors (Fullard, 2023). This is not a affirmative statement. We might conclude that many organisations in the wider economy *should* function more like schools—in their commitment to core values, in their respect for employee rights, in their prioritisation of staff welfare, and in other ways. As a practical matter, however, law firms, banks, architectural practices, professional services firms, technology companies and other organisations have quite different expectations of their staff than are commonly found in schools. In some areas of the curriculum, this dilemma is well recognised and well addressed. Most high-performing music, art and drama departments are staffed by teachers who remain actively engaged with their creative practice. Many teachers of physical education play competitive sport to a high level or will have done until the stage of life when competition becomes more challenging (and often, well beyond that point).

Skills and competencies

It is therefore essential that employers have some input into the design of careers education as well as its execution. At the LAE, the first step in this journey was to understand employability in terms of a balance between skills and competencies. There is a rich academic literature in both education and management theory drawing the distinction between skills and competencies. Typically, skills are defined in functional terms related to the effective execution of a specific role—coding, handling accounts, etc.—while competencies are defined more broadly as knowledge, understanding and behaviours that lead to the successful performance of a wider variety of roles—analytical thinking and negotiating prowess are often cited as examples of competencies. The LAE's leadership was certainly aware of this literature and of the importance of the central distinction between skills and competencies, but the real reason for focusing on both when revising the school's careers education programme was more prosaic: we talked to employers, and they were universally clear that

both should be explicit objects of effective careers education. The LAE is fortunate in having strong relationships with many employers. These relationships
are undoubtedly helped by the school's location in the East End of London,
close to the City, to banks, fund managers and law firms, to multinationals with
headquarters or significant local offices, to central government, and to several
hospital trusts. The school does not yet have an alumni network in positions of
seniority in those employers—although that day is not far off—but it benefits
from connections that are made possible by its independent school partners. It
is important to acknowledge these advantages but also to stress the importance
of the use to which the LAE has put them.

Aspirations and shifting preferences

The second, no less essential element of an effective careers education programme is an understanding of the school's students, their aspirations and eventual destinations. Through semi-annual student and alumni surveys, induction
procedures, parent interviews and careers guidance sessions, all data points indicate that the LAE serves a highly aspirational community. For a variety of local
reasons, those aspirations are drawn in quite conventional ways. Which is to
say that LAE students typically join the school with quite specific views of the
careers to which they aspire but without detailed knowledge of those careers.
Parental expectations and the local schools landscape are both at work here. The
LAE community, as has been repeatedly observed, includes a high percentage
of young people who are able to trace their family history to South Asia and,
to a lesser extent, West Africa and Eastern Europe. National datasets indicate
that these communities have high regard for formal education and for specific
professions closely associated with formal education. On the other hand, East
London includes a very significant number of secondary schools without sixth
forms. Much commentary on careers education in secondary schools that stop at
age 16 focuses on the reduced incentives such schools have had to invest scarce
resources in careers education since the official school leaving age was raised
to 18. We prefer to focus on the practical challenges that secondary schools face
in developing the sort of direct relationships with employees across a sufficient
range of sectors to really refine their careers offer. Be that as it may, in a typical
year, perhaps 40% of students joining the LAE in Year 12 will tell their teachers
that they want to go to medical school and become a doctor. The next most popular career choices relate to finance, the law, engineering, computer science and
technology. Only a handful of students in any given cohort will have any first-
hand contact with any of those professions (with the obvious, notable exception
of having visited the family doctor). Very few students recall significant guidance
having been provided by their secondary school. Of course, LAE students, like
sixth formers everywhere, go on a journey of discovery about themselves and

their place in the wider world. To make the obvious point, 40% of students do *not* go on to attend a medical school. (In a typical year, the actual figure is around 15%, which is broadly in line with the number of students who go on to study at Oxford or Cambridge.) Nonetheless, this is mostly a question of shifting preferences within a well-defined opportunity set. The sectors which recur most often in students' initial interviews in Year 12 *are* the sectors in which most LAE alumni are working today.[1] There are sadly not many schools operating in areas of high deprivation where students initially aspiring to a medical career learn to love the law, but that is exactly the course traced by one of the LAE's highest-performing students in its current Year 13 cohort.

The qualities essential for success

A school with a good understanding of its students and positive relationships with employers can form a bridge between the two. The LAE conducted a thorough review of its careers programme in 2022 (see box on the LAE Diploma). The first step in this review was to identify those skills and competencies that were in greatest demand by employers in those sectors in which LAE students typically aspire to build careers. Given the ethnic make-up of the LAE's student body, the school had to take seriously the specific challenges that British students from minority groups, as well as those from working-class homes, were likely to face in the workplace and the competencies needed successfully to navigate those experiences. The school organised focus groups, conducted structured interviews, surveys and longer discussions to identify the competencies that the employers valued most in their workforces. The school was fortunate in its timing. The public conversation about inclusion, smouldering for too long at the margins of academia and in the NGO sector, had broken into a wildfire throughout the public and private sectors as a result of the activism of the Black Lives Matter, MeToo and EveryOneInvited movements, among others. Many larger employers were reflecting on the need to diversify their workforce and to revisit employment practices that allowed for the exercise of implicit bias or explicit discrimination. As the Director of People at a large insurance company said: 'Every company in the FTSE 100 is taking a long hard look at its talent management strategy. And every company needs to.' This period of introspection made for open, productive conversations with senior executives about the qualities they most valued in early career professionals. Several companies were prepared to

---

1 There are, of course, a good number of LAE students with quite different aspirations and alumni in diverse careers not covered in this passage. The list is not meant to signify any hierarchy of aspiration or to assign any greater social value to one career versus another. Nonetheless, the point holds.

host 'think ins', moderated by the LAE Headteacher, at which professionals at different career stages reflected on those qualities that are most essential for success. The timing also had a practical benefit. Several employers had carried out or commissioned proprietary research into their workforces' attitude to work which they were prepared to share on a confidential basis with the school. A final, crucial element was the active involvement of the LAE alumni building careers in engineering, finance, health, the law, professional services and technology. These former students' voices were crucial in securing the integrity of the research. As one consultant specialising in organisational change said: 'There may be a more profound generation gap in the workplace than at any time in history. Both the impact of technology and culture change mean that younger people have fundamentally different expectations and are having a fundamentally different experience in their early careers than the people they look to as mentors.' In short, the voices of early-career professionals are essential to ensure the relevance of the research.

The output of the research was the LAE Career Essentials: a list of eight skills and competencies that are most relevant to young people seeking to build careers in the sectors listed above. The elements of the Framework, along with brief examples of what each element might mean in practice, is shown in Table 7.1.

As a relatively recent invention, the LAE does not yet have robust evidence of how effective the Essentials are as a scaffold to the development of employability skills. A robust impact assessment is planned for the coming school year. The Framework has been incorporated into the LAE Diploma, a core part of the school's provision, and sits alongside the government's Gatsby Benchmarks as a vital guide to the development of effective careers education. In some ways, the Framework and the Benchmarks pose similar challenges. In both cases, a critical challenge is to normalise the inclusion of 'careers content' in 'regular' lessons. The LAE has established the initial conditions for success by incorporating careers education prominently in its Learning Essentials (see Chapter 5). Routinely revisiting both documents in departmental and heads of subject meetings to check on progress and to share best practice is an essential part of the embedding process. Perhaps the most important active ingredient is high but reasonable expectations. Some skills and competencies are more easily developed in some subjects than others. As a reasonable generalisation, history lessons offer a greater opportunity to study and emulate inspiring communication than they do digital citizenship. Physics lessons, likewise, may not be silent on the topic of developing cultural compass, but they are replete with opportunities to develop superior communications skills. As in so many areas of school provision, achieving consistency in this area does not mean everyone doing the same thing so much as it means everyone working towards a common goal, according to a common set of standards. In a spirit of candour, it is worth pointing out that, while the LAE and many other schools have developed significant expertise in many areas of careers education, most continue to struggle

Table 7.1: The LAE Career Essentials

1. Inspiring Communication

   - Eloquent speaker and presenter
   - Clear and concise writer
   - Conveyor of contagious energy

2. Superior Quantification

   - Financially literate
   - Proficient in statistical analysis
   - Data scientist

3. Relationship Building

   - Emotionally intelligent colleague
   - Generous, effective team player
   - Active network builder

4. Independent Research

   - Curious and eager learner
   - Relentless pursuer of relevant information and evidence
   - Critical interpreter

5. Cultural Compass

   - Celebrator of cultural diversity
   - Skilled diplomat
   - Proficient in a second language

6. Digital Citizenship

   - Sophisticated and responsible user of social media
   - Proficient user of key productivity tools
   - Coder

7. Entrepreneurial Mindset

   - Intrinsically motivated
   - Strategic thinker and planner
   - Agile and effective change agent

8. Authentic Leadership

   - Morally centred and values-driven
   - Disciplined and self-efficacious
   - Able to influence and inspire others

to sustain an informed dialogue with their students about the importance of entrepreneurialism. Too many young people still leave school convinced that the only viable way to make a living or build a career is by working for someone else. This is something the LAE hopes to address over the coming years.

The LAE Diploma

The LAE has offered its Diploma course alongside core A-level provision almost since the school was founded in 2012. For most of that time, the Diploma offered a means by which teachers could encourage and track students' participation in co-curricular activities. The Diploma also served as a vehicle through which students could evidence how their engagement with a wider set of opportunities could contribute to the development of habits of mind and body that would make them successful university students.

At its most ambitious, the Diploma was a highly effective framework for character education. Put more bluntly, the Diploma got students working towards a successful UCAS application almost from the moment they arrived in the school. The Diploma was inspired by similar schemes that were well established in some of the LAE's partner independent schools, such as Brighton College and Forest School, but its design principles would be familiar to many maintained schools.

In 2021, the LAE leadership began to take a long, hard look at the Diploma. The stimulus for this review was partly the return to in-person schooling after a period of unprecedented disruption brought about by school closures designed to help combat the Covid-19 pandemic. As in every other setting subject to government-mandated closure, the LAE was forced to adapt much of its provision so that learning could take place predominantly online. That which could not be adapted, had to be suspended. Complete suspension was thankfully rare, but fell more heavily on the co-curricular programme than on the core curriculum. Unsurprisingly, sailing is more difficult than maths lessons to turn into an enriching online experience.

The school leadership also took note of raised government expectations regarding careers education, information, advice and guidance trialled throughout 2021 and introduced into Ofsted's *Further Education Inspection Framework* in summer 2022 (Ofsted, 2022). These expectations placed greater weight on the responsibilities that sixth form schools and colleges bear to prepare students for the world of work. The expectations were framed very much in terms of 'workplace skills', although, for reasons explored below, the school leadership felt this was too narrow a conceptualisation. The LAE was in the fortunate position that its existing Pathways programme was already well adapted to the increased government expectations (reflecting, in part, we fully accept, the school's favourable location in East London, close to many highly prestigious employers). But compliance is hardly excellence.

Finally, the school is committed to a culture of continuous improvement. The Diploma had served a useful function for several years, helping to develop and cement students' understanding of the LAE's core values—Excellence, Independence, Integrity, Respect, Resilience and Humility. But no system is meant to last forever. For all these reasons, the time was ripe to revisit the Diploma.

The objective, therefore, was to re-imagine the LAE Diploma in a way that gave greater weight and increased structure to careers education, while recognising that schools' moral responsibility extends beyond the 'production' of effective employees, executives or entrepreneurs and includes the cultivation of responsible citizens, community members and neighbours.

The first step in revising the Diploma was the development of the LAE Career Essentials (see Table 7.1). The Framework established important success criteria for students working towards the LAE Diploma. It gave the Diploma a focus on performance character, although not by abandoning its focus on moral character. Over the course of the first four terms at the LAE, students compile evidence of progress towards developing at least four of the eight skills and competencies included in the framework. Evidence can be accumulated by taking part in activities in school, activities organised by the school and activities that the student organises independently. The latter is a key differentiator; for example, it is hard to accumulate evidence of an entrepreneurial mindset by doing only those things that other people have organised for you.

A key change to the Diploma was to require students to engage actively with several different career paths. Prior to 2022, the LAE had been in the fortunate position of being able to offer its students an extensive range of opportunities to develop understanding of rich and rewarding careers. This took the form of the school's Pathways programme, through which all students gained weekly access to guest speakers from different companies and sectors; through its annual Futures Fair, attended by more than 50 employers and universities; through work placements and internships during the Easter and summer recesses; and through the embedding of careers education in the core curriculum as one of the LAE Learning Essentials.

However, the design of the programme was permissive. Students with an interest in a specific career path could, in theory, continually revisit that career path in all of the ways just listed without seriously engaging with a potential alternative. This did seem to meet the demands of a rounded careers education.

The LAE Diploma now requires students to evidence their investigation of three sectors as potential sites to build a career. In some cases, these sectors may be related: for example, a would-be doctor could reasonably investigate medical technology as one of their three options. But students must also evidence engagement with a diversity of alternative careers. So, the same would-be doctor could not meet the demands of the Diploma by choosing medical research as a third option. The law or engineering, both clearly different fields, would be a more suitable choice.

The requirement to investigate a variety of different career options has also proven a constructive challenge to the school's provision. Students who were asked to feed into the development of the revised Diploma rightly pointed out that those whose interests lay more in the social sciences were less well served by the LAE careers programme than those studying STEM (Science, Technology, Engineering, and, Mathematics) subjects. The school leadership responded by increasing the number of opportunities to learn about careers in the law, the civil service, journalism and other fields.

Mentoring programme

People already active in the workplace should also be involved more directly in helping to develop students' understanding of the careers open to them. Access to professional mentors can change lives, particularly for Disadvantaged students who are unlikely to have family connections in the professions. The LAE has established a network of professional mentors who work intensively with students in a year-long programme. The school's medium-term aspiration is that every enrolled student should have a professional mentor. In the near term, in keeping with its mission to combat educational disadvantaged and advance social mobility, the LAE prioritises students who are Disadvantaged when allocating mentors. Mapping mentors to students is a complex process. In all cases, the matching is carried out by the school based on information provided by both mentor and student and to avoid the introduction of any unconscious bias. Many key considerations involve balancing the availability of mentors with the aspirations and preferences of students. The scheme is not yet sufficiently mature that the school can in every case pair a student with someone working in the sector to which they aspire. There are persuasive arguments on both sides regarding whether this would even be best practice—particularly considering the school's aim to broaden its students' perspective on potential careers. A more practical limitation in the school's context is that the availability of mentors reflects the current composition of specific sectors. In practice, it means that mentors represent quite different demographic groups from the students they are supporting. This reflects the nature of professional employment in the UK. Most students are sensitive to this fact and understand the benefits that come from working with an experienced professional who can help them to shape their career aspirations. This is not to say that they would not, in some cases, prefer to be working with someone with whom they can more immediately identify based on personal characteristics such as ethnicity, faith or gender. But students tend to understand that professional life involves learning to build productive relationships across axes of difference. More often than not, they take much the same approach to their teachers. The LAE is increasingly using its growing alumni network to provide students with a parallel source of insight closer to their own lived experience (see below).

The LAE is very clear with both students and mentors that their relationship is professional and 'curated' by the school.[2] Practically, mentors are paired with three students at a time. Although the school requires that mentors undergo checking by the Disclosure and Barring Service, one-on-one mentoring relationships are not permitted. Mentors commit to meeting students four times per year, a minimum of twice in person, the first of which is facilitated by an in-school launch event to which all mentors are invited. Subsequent in-person meetings can be organised at the school or at the mentor's place of business, based on availability. The LAE does not authorise

---

2   The LAE, like any responsible school, takes its safeguarding responsibilities incredibly seriously.

in-person meetings in other locations. Online meetings are organised via Microsoft Teams using the school's account. The school provides mentors with an adaptable 'script' for the first meeting, which is designed to establish priorities for subsequent sessions, and guidance on the appropriate scope for mentoring throughout the process. Mentors can, and many do, increase the number of meetings with students but are asked to log this with the school. Many of the other protocols that govern the mentoring relationship are designed to normalise the experience of dealing with more experienced or senior professionals.

The burden of administration is heaped on the student mentees. Mentors are asked to indicate times when they can be available based on information provided about the school timetable. Student mentees are responsible for their own attendance, punctuality and, if meetings are held online, for organising the exchange of links. Mentors are asked to report any lateness or non-attendance by student mentees, which can quickly result in the student being withdrawn from the scheme. Students are asked to keep meeting logs, including any actions agreed with mentors, and to revisit those actions at the start of subsequent meetings. Both students and mentors are given strict communication protocols to which they are expected to adhere. As LAE students are (separately) taught to develop LinkedIn profiles, that platform is preferred. School and office emails can be shared, personal emails may not. Mentors are asked not to give out their mobile phone numbers, even if this is a 'work' phone that belongs to their employer. Mentors and mentees are also given clear guidance to expect that their relationship is time-bounded, although, as a practical matter, LAE students quickly become adults and move on to university or into degree-awarding employment. The school cannot rule out the development of longer-term mentor–mentee relationships arising out of its programme in the same way they could arise out of any other professional interaction.

Conclusion and leadership takeaways

This chapter has dealt with how the LAE prepares students for the richest, most rewarding degree and degree-equivalent courses and, ultimately, careers. To rephrase the slightly blunt assessment of the Minister of Education from the start of this chapter, the quality of student destinations is perhaps the single most objective measure of a school's effectiveness. School leaders can treat it as such by allocating resources in support of destination planning. High-performing students will need a solid foundation of academic excellence, opportunities to explore their academic interests well beyond their A-level lessons, specialist preparation for any admissions process to be undertaken and plentiful opportunities to meet the graduates and professionals whose path they aspire to trace. Some families can support their children in all those respects; for those who cannot, schools can act as the launching pad for happy, successful adult lives.

Reference

Fullard, J. (2023) Invalid estimates and biased means: a replication of a recent meta-analysis investigating the effect of teacher professional development on pupil outcomes. *Social Sciences & Humanities Open*, 8(1), 100605.

8
Exploring Our DNA of Partnership Working

At the core of the LAE is genuine, deep-seated partnership. We began as the unique product of a collaboration between six of the UK's leading independent schools, which had a shared drive to increase social mobility through improving access to the top universities in some of the UK's most deprived boroughs. As a result, these schools–Brighton College, Caterham School, Eton College, Forest School, Highgate School and University College School–are woven into the DNA and structure of our state school. Each House is linked to, and named after, one of them. These Houses visit their associated schools to get to know their sixth form 'buddies' there. LAE sixth formers then host their buddies when they come to Stratford. This has proven to be a great learning experience, with pupils at both establishments discovering what they have in common and how they can learn from each other. It also introduces LAE students to a group of new contacts outside their immediate environment, which have proven useful in their future careers. Education is substantially more than the passing of exams and our close relationship with these top independent schools greatly enhances and extends the range of opportunities on offer to our students and they benefit from experiences they would perhaps never have expected.

Four quadrants of partnership

As part of our partnership strategy, we divided partnerships into four quadrants, namely curriculum, academic, co-curricular and development, as shown in Figure 8.1.

Curriculum partnership e.g. teach meets, action research, CPD	**Academic partnership** e.g. lectures, reading programmes, trips and visits
Co-curricular partnership e.g. sports, debating, performing arts	**Development partnership** e.g. direct financial support, support with funding applications

Figure 8.1   The four quadrants of partnership

The basic expectation that the LAE has is that our core partner schools are involved in all four quadrants. We still have productive relationships with many other schools in any one of these quadrants—we mention some of them at the end of this chapter—but from our perspective that is quite different from a genuine partnership.

We will be considering in this chapter the issues that we have discovered have an impact on the longer-term sustainability of school partnerships, and exploring how easily what works in partnerships can be made into a transferable set of principles and ideas to guide other schools in this type of venture.

What have we found to be the benefits of working in close partnership?

As we hope to show, our own model of Independent and State School Partnership (ISSP) has been an invaluable asset to the LAE. Some of the significant advantages we have discovered over a decade are here offered in more detail, with wider observations that will hopefully explain why we have continued, and with renewed commitment, the collaborations that kick-started our school.

First, our partnerships have enabled all of the contributing schools to *harness the general strengths from both sectors*. There is little doubt that the Ofsted-driven environment in many state schools directs teachers towards gaining student motivation and commitment through grade inducements as well as teaching to the test. That is not to say that the state sector doesn't deserve credit for its emphasis on adaptive pedagogy, but there are dangers in confusing specification knowledge for subject knowledge. There is perhaps an increasing risk that, as more and more MATs (Multi Academy Trusts) develop teams dedicated to curriculum development, they may actually de-skill 'regular' classroom teachers. Independent school teachers have commented on their greater access to out-of-class enrichment and beyond-syllabus activities that can lead to a wider perspective on learning. The independent sector often assumes a much higher degree of engagement from their students (and their heavily financially committed parents), so the long and winding road to scholarship is often better supported. Given the obvious advantages (and concerns) regarding both these approaches, a shared arena where these can be discussed, innovative cross-sector ideas formulated and strategies implemented has surely and inevitably benefitted the target group that matters the most: namely, our students. In both sectors.

A second success we have found has been *the cross-pollination of subject-based solutions* driven through collaboration. The overriding aim of partnership must be to learn together, to ask what can be learned from each other, and this has engendered a genuinely reciprocal approach. This is turn has helped to deepen and strengthen our relationships, making the partnerships at the heart of our approach more sustainable and has helped to ensure a genuine sense of fairness and equity. The harsh reality is that there can be a resentment from the state sector about the supposed 'easier life' of independent schools, combined with the sense that as a sector, we really don't have much to learn from the exercise of privilege. Specifically, many state schools question if the approaches used in independent schools would have much relevance to their own students in their own far less advantaged context. When this is combined with a hesitancy among some independent schoolteachers about being seen to tell state school colleagues where they might be going wrong, the resulting partnership can be irretrievably skewed. We have found these speculations to be profoundly untrue. All schools involved in a reciprocal partnership must have as much to gain from one another as they have to share. We have seen that it is when subject teachers from both sectors get together to discuss what problems they actually face that real dialogue happens. At this point it becomes far clearer that there is much to be gained by exploring and addressing some of our shared annoyances (such as frustration with exam board unreliability, anger at ill-informed government whims, increasingly poor examination specifications – we freely acknowledge that the mutual 'challenges' list can be surprisingly long).

A third benefit has been *to share understanding of what actually works* within our respective schools. It can be that many schools have surprisingly skewed ideas of what they actually do exceptionally well, so having close connections and observations from 'outside' their usual sphere of influence can reveal unacknowledged or even unknown interesting practice. All schools, no matter what sector they work in, have blind spots. It has been quite an eye opener to understand what each of the schools involved in our partnership really can offer. A school might believe it has particular expertise in an area and that therefore becomes the initial focus of help and support. This can be misguided, or may address a need that another school may not consider to be that useful to them. School self-reporting of strengths and weaknesses can be misleading, but through collaboration, it can be substantially improved. In addition, it is not always easy to see delineation along state and independent school lines. For example, there are many practices and views shared across institutional type, particularly when schools are teaching to the same subject specification. So by triangulating data from staff and student surveys, lesson research observations, exchange activities and professional networks, we have seen a far more accurate picture emerging of some of the similarities and differences between the two sectors. We have as a result all benefitted from this honest engagement with the ideas and thinking of others, and seeing practice through the eyes of an outsider.

Our last partnership gain is possibly the most profound, namely *the deepening of exam and subject knowledge* in students and staff across all schools. State teachers readily concede that there is far too little time offered by their schools with regard to maintaining or improving their own subject expertise and knowledge. Senior leadership in state schools tend to prioritise exam board-based professional development. As a result, they often have a far clearer view of what is required by exam boards. Working from a broad but defensible generalisation, the independent sector tends to pride itself on teacher subject knowledge, often prioritising this over teacher pedagogy. This opens up an interesting area where both sectors can support and steer the other, if the mechanisms are in place to allow this to happen. Cross-sector subject-specific development days offer chances to share strategies, resources and approaches, and to establish an agreed empirically-informed basis from which to work. The expertise that resides in the independent sector is clear and is far wider than a simple understanding of further maths or Latin and classics, because these schools happen to teach many more students on these slightly more selective courses. Independent school teachers typically have a greater wealth of experience dealing with larger groups of high-ability students, which means that they often have a far clearer idea of what these courses demand at the very top end. They also have a clearer sense of the kinds of students who are capable of achieving these top grades, as most state schools see substantially smaller numbers of such students so it is far harder to know what can be expected from such students. The act of co-developing and trialling resources for such students, as has happened with an English 'taster' course based on threshold concepts, is an example of an easy win to all schools involved.

What are the key principles sitting behind the LAE partnerships?

Working with so many leading independent schools on such a variety of pro-grammes has enabled us to consider what really sits behind a successful partnership. What follows are eight of the conclusions we have come to. As we have so many ongoing partnership activities at any one time, ranging from the UCS jazz ensemble to working with Forest School Combined Cadet Force to Brighton College offering economics master classes, we have tried to illustrate each of the principles below using just one programme, to clarify what they look like in practice. The one we chose is the Eton & London Academy of Excellence Leadership Institute (ELLI) programme. Broadly, the course consisted of various activities throughout the year related to character development in leadership.

Wider aims

First, it is vitally important from the start to *establish the wider aims*. Partner-ship itself is not an aim. Nor is giving something back, satisfying government priorities or raising school profiles locally. Nor is encouraging social cohesion, self-esteem, friendships, networking or student wellbeing. Lovely as these ide-als are, such levels of vagueness serve no one well. Similarly, improving the attainment, aspirations and ambitions of less advantaged students is a noble cause, but if these are the result of insufficient teaching time, large classes and poor or patchy prior attainment, what realistically will a partnership be able to do to help? The wider aims can be highly ambitious, such as improving social mobility, but they need to be chunked into a form that is achievable and meas-urable. If these aims are closely tied to addressing known curriculum deficits or extra-curricular developments that could tangentially improve results, then they will undoubtedly be of greater immediate value to teachers.

This search for purpose needs to be based on a sound and secure under-standing of the specific issues being faced in the schools involved. *Looking at the values that each school holds dear, and seeing where a natural fit may occur, is a central tenet and the underlying architecture of successful partner-ships.* Without this understanding and alignment, relationships can become forced. A useful question to take forward is: What more does a school wish to achieve? If possible, a programme should be trialled across both sectors and lead to direct benefits to learners. If the initiative is seen to be a positive, is it also seen to be equally impactful in all of the schools engaging with it? To what extent could it be a transferable or scalable asset?

In summary, explicit and clear aims need to be ascertained at the very out-set, preferably with agreement across the senior management teams and ide-ally governing bodies of the schools involved. Ideally, this should also form part of a school's wider strategic development plan, so that the longer-term sustainability of the programme is considered. With the ELLI initiative, the wider aims were twofold. The first was to extend the Year 12 curriculum offer to include character and leadership development, and in so doing secure a measurable increase in participants' character virtues, leadership understand-ing and practice, and improved academic outcomes. The second was to pro-vide the evidence and practical tools for other schools to use in extending their own curriculum offering to include character development.

Adaptation built in

This leads on to the next principle, which is *to ensure the point of the pro-gramme can be adapted*. What worked at the start of a project or a partner-ship, and genuinely benefitted the cohorts or schools involved, may in itself have meant that the schools do not need that type of intervention any longer. This is a significant positive. In any successful partnership, the support given should have developed the capacity of the schools involved to be able to run similar interventions without the direct assistance that might once have been needed. *Change is inevitable, and needs to be recognised, so that a partner-ship is not seen to be meeting expressed needs that may have been relevant from years before, that have now radically shifted, or been met.* In addition, if the initiating schools have benefitted from the programme or partnership, are there ways that new schools or a wider cohort of students can be brought on board? What are the factors that might be significant to enable transferability or scalability? Obviously there are some dangers in widening a partnership or shifting the focus of a programme (to name a few, the dissipation of energies, potential conflicts of interest, changing the baseline measures) but there are also huge potential gains (testing of ideas in a new environment, different sets of expertise to be accessed, more learners benefitting). There needs to be an upfront agreement as to who is given the power to agree or to veto approaches from other schools and to clarify procedures to shift the balance and focus of the programme or partnership as and when it is needed. So a useful question any partnership should be asking themselves from the very beginning has to be: What developments might be next? Planning in quite formal opportunities to revisit the 'What next?' question at a project level is key. Perhaps there is a need for an annual exercise revisiting the extent to which the partnership is meeting its overall objectives, closely followed by how best to capture processes, rather than just narrative descriptions, to try to preserve the authentic voice of the educators and learners to enable practice to be understood as it is.

In summary, procedures need to be put in place that allow for further modifications, expansions and developments to the programme agreement, baked in from the start, which set out the means and requirements through which this can be achieved. With the ELLI initiative, it meant keeping a close focus on what are the interesting questions, issues and practice? Where were these in action? What useful mistakes have been made and what has been learned from these? What have been the unintended consequences and what can be learned from these? How do we locate what is best about our own practice, and develop the confidence and the language base to more effectively engage in professional dialogue? Ultimately we are looking for:

- What success could look like (such as the creation of a Leadership Institute which is attended by all students, a more explicit discussion about leadership understanding and practice, inviting guest speakers from more diverse backgrounds and experiences and a better use of technology to support the programme).
- What the key ingredients were (offering opportunities to hear the views and exchange ideas with those from different schools or backgrounds), where these fell short of expectations (the need for mutuality of commitment, timetabling issues and the use of an online environment in a more effective way).
- How the best aspects could be captured and ultimately replicated (research support for collecting data, admin and teacher support to deliver the programme).

Clarify gains

A common mistake is not being specific enough when setting up a programme about the benefits to the school (staff and students) and the demands that will be made. It is important *to clarify with colleagues about what the school or cohort will actually gain by getting involved.* Initial teacher outcomes from partnership programmes tend to impact only on the professional development of the teachers immediately involved, and through them, to the students in their classes. This is important. *But in the longer term this CPD needs to be considerably extended, into becoming school-wide outcomes, through peer-to-peer teaching and in-house 'up-skilling' so that capacity is built and all staff are kept on board.* It is important to have actively sought and canvassed the views of the Heads of Department and subject teachers. To support this idea, the LAE surveys staff at least three times annually on a range of issues and often conducts *ad hoc* surveys on specific topics. Regular staff (and student) surveys may also help this process at the very beginning and, more significantly, when pressures have increased. In any event, motivation and engagement will vary across the project as increased workloads and time commitments take their toll. Partnerships have an awkward way of impacting on many colleagues across a school who might not seem to be directly involved, via increased cover arrangements and classes not taught. So surveys need to cover the whole school in order to gain a clearer understanding about what and why sacrifices may need to be made in the longer term. This is particularly important to ensure that key members of the programme are not over-stretched, out of school too much or resented by other colleagues who may be asked to cover for them. Once initial suspicions are dispelled, it is a significant feature of successful partnerships that there is a genuine desire to continue learning from one another. There is also a professional curiosity aroused to see first-hand how other schools deal with similar issues. Co-teaching in one another's schools can really help to break down barriers, as it begins to establish commonalities, a better understanding of context, empathy and, most importantly, a relationship with and between students. Additionally, the joint development of resources and joint inset delivery are also powerful bonding activities as they encourage useful dependencies. Following up on the basis of the findings from the partnership outcomes requires further interventions, which are designed to replicate the factors that were seen to work, testing them in different contexts and spreading the benefit across the school.

To summarise, what colleagues and students across the schools will get from the arrangements needs to be made explicit at the start, not in terms of any quick fixes or social plaudits, but rather in terms of how the programme will benefit staff and students, and preferably also build capacity across the schools and establishing how this will be enacted to benefit the wider staff community. The ELLI initiative led to an empowered student cohort in terms of confidence. Students had opportunities to prepare and deliver presentations to unfamiliar audiences, and engage in wider reading from academic sources outside the subject specific. For the staff involved, it enabled them to see how their students rose to challenges, dealt with differing circumstances, and struggled and achieved in environments in which they weren't usually tested. It enabled both groups to see what life looked like out of their respective school bubbles.

Trust

It is easy in education to assume that goodwill is in endless supply, but it is essential to *build honesty and transparency into the partnership* in very clear and explicit steps. Trust is vital for working through the operational difficulties that inevitably arise. A clear understanding from the outset about what participation will tangibly involve helps to build that trust. Retaining the key people remains essential to successful partnership working between schools. The task for continuing partnerships will always be to further embed it into school life. There is no substitute for regular, ongoing dialogue, but it is useful to consider how dialogue can be supplemented by a formal memorandum of understanding setting out what the schools will achieve from the relationship and requirements to fulfil the needs and expectations of all. The memorandum of understanding should also cover and shape realistic but ambitious goals, accounting for sufficient staff time and resources. Without this top level of institutional 'buy in', relationships, no matter how resilient, may collapse. It is far too easy to underestimate how much time and commitment will be needed to ensure a successful partnership. Err on the generous side. Early investment is key. Front load the time to enable the communication to happen before the partnership starts, in the first few weeks and months. The benefits will be reaped later. Getting schools to enter into partnerships can be irksome in the extreme, but continuation of the network into the longer term is far harder. *The driving force remains the attitude and values of staff initiating, running and organising the partnerships, and so the decision on which schools to collaborate with is critical.* Schools should share the same values and enthusiasm for partnership working, as without them partnerships can dissolve into amorphous, one-off type collaborations (sharing playing fields, swimming pools and physics teachers) that are only really useful for local PR drives. Clarity and honesty are key drivers here.

In summary, thought needs to be given to how the hearts and minds agenda becomes central to the moral purpose of the relationship between colleagues from the two sectors. What are the best ways to develop commonality, openness, inclusiveness and professional dialogue? What are the key benefits that need to be recognised from the outset? What are the pitfalls? How can each school bring their individual and sector-based expertise to the table? With the ELLI initiative, this involved the programme being trialled across both schools involved, so that it was not seen to be something that one school already did well and therefore was the expert source. Colleagues from both schools were involved from the outset, building on the good relationships that had already been built up between the two schools through their mutual engagements with The Tony Little Centre for Innovation and Research in Learning (CIRL), where the Heads and Governors and researchers met on a termly basis to discuss innovation and partnership. Their lead researcher was well known to all the colleagues involved and her professionalism was implicitly trusted. The Deputy Head from the LAE was involved from the very start in the design of the programme and was also the lead teacher in the activities that took place.

This high-level Senior Leadership Team buy-in was a significant factor to the initial success and therefore the continuation of the programme itself.

Needs met

Another principle that is often neglected is ensuring that the schools involved have managed to *locate a key element of difficulty that actually needs addressing*. Assumptions made without clear evidence are dangerous, and unfortunately rife in partnership working. There is often a touching assumption of a universal yet usually unspoken sense of fairness and equity as the driving force behind any network. However, the key to success is ensuring that the partnership is seen to be meeting genuine needs that all the schools involved have agreed will require addressing. *These need to involve honest, specific and sometimes difficult conversations about what students might be missing and what issues colleagues are therefore facing day to day in their own classrooms*. Colleagues have to focus on what isn't working, and why. Insecurities can be around teaching complex topics, the lack of wider non-curricular opportunities, poor grasp of top-end assessment, inadequate cultural capital, exam board inconsistencies, fear about neglecting the broader development of students, or a host of other issues. The creation of rich student activities can lead on to significant CPD opportunities, and incredibly powerful and potentially long-lasting gains for teachers, such as encouraging them to reflect on their own and their peers' practices, developing thinking or renewing passion and enthusiasm for their teaching. It is additionally handy if commitment to the partnership can help schools to meet some of the targets set by their own school development plans or their wider learning aims. This can be examined and incorporated, if approached flexibly and pragmatically, at the early stages of the planned programme. Only then can a focus be found that looks at genuine challenges faced and how these might be best addressed across the sectors.

In summary, establishing what the real challenges are that are being faced by students and teachers in the schools involved is key. It will often involve a deeper understanding of educational pressures across the wider area, or the type of institution, and then developing plans that might directly address them. With the ELLI initiative, this emerged as preparation for leaving school, taking responsibility and preparing for university. Students mentioned that the opportunity to work with others was really beneficial for them and equipped them with the necessary skills for university, and subsequently at work. For some of the students who wanted to go into careers in medicine or to work in multinational businesses, they believed the teamworking skills were vital for them and the programme had a positive benefit. Students also commented on the reading of challenging texts from academic sources as good preparation for university as it enabled them to grapple with concepts they were not familiar with.

Outcomes

Although it might seem premature at the start, it is extremely useful to consider what the specific partnership outcomes might be. As an example, simply frontloading immediate benefits encourages confidence in the ability of the partnership to get things completed. So at the beginning, it is always useful to hit a few 'low hanging fruit' outcomes, to motivate continued engagement and involvement. Such successes convince schools that it is in their interest to persevere when the harder outcomes require greater efforts. It is vital that there is a transparent degree of honesty in recording outcomes. Many will not be met, or at least, not demonstrably met. They may be too ambitious or difficult to isolate due to a small sample size or poor attendance. Often in education, there is no control group. Some outcomes are high profile and offer recognition for efforts and immediate publicity, but how these are managed and assessed matters. *It is also useful to consider if all the schools involved in the partnership are sharing the plaudits, and if the inevitably uneven resources available across the network are properly taken into account and publicly recognised.* If not, resentment may build quietly behind the scenes. Often the key difference is in the specificity of outcome. In schools with little experience of applying for top universities or where the sixth form pastoral team is inexperienced, for example, it is highly unlikely that students will get effective support with the nuts and bolts of the applications that they make. However, independent schools can easily help this process, particularly in terms of the quality of the students' Personal Statements. The will needs to be there to seek that support, even if only in the pursuit of equity and fairness. But there is a qualitative step change between '*working together to help build confidence with university interviews*' and setting up detailed preparation approaches to tests that vary according to subject (in law – LNAT (Law National Aptitude Test), in medicine – BMAT (BioMedical Admissions Test), etc.), followed by targeted interview practice depending on which university or college a student is applying to. One requires some expertise and a general feeling of supporting colleagues in less advantaged schools. The other involves highly specific interventions which are tailored and personalised.

To summarise, in order to keep a programme on track, there needs to be an agreed process where the outcomes are honestly examined, assessed, redefined and widened as necessary, with clear teaching and learning outcomes linked to evaluative measures. With the ELLI initiative, it was found after careful analysis that the programme had no statistically significant difference for any of the five character traits that were measured. Given that the students who took part in ELLI were a self-selecting group, it is possible that they were already engaged with issues of leadership and, as such, had a nuanced understanding of what it means to be a leader (some of the scores in the pre-programme surveys were already quite high). On the other hand, the students who took part in ELLI performed better in their A-level results and comparable end-of-year exams, as well as being accepted at elite universities. This was particularly true for students on free school meals who took part in ELLI compared to those who did not. There were also perceived benefits in increased confidence, understanding of leadership, academic challenge, and learning about the viewpoints of other students.

Scrutiny

Another question that needs to be addressed is whether to *commit to an independent stand-alone or an internal scrutiniser.* Should the partnership body be guided only by the wider school management teams or by an external agency? The dangers of scrutiny being 'in house' is that there are obvious vested interests in the programme being seen to be successful, particularly if the team involved is also the team evaluating. Investment has been made and the 'sunk cost' fallacy raises its head. Outsiders to the network can act as significant critical friends who are often better placed to see any potential areas where conflicts of interest may arise, and this wider involvement can prove to be effective for helping to ensure project fidelity in terms of delivery and approaches taken. Any partnership needs to be run efficiently to keep colleagues engaged. Notes, minutes, meetings, negotiations, timetabling and agendas don't sort themselves. Inevitably there will need to be an individual or a committee that is tasked with driving this utterly necessary administration. An independent body can usefully keep an ongoing eye as to whether the partnership is becoming too dependent on a small number of stalwarts who have taken on more than their fair share of responsibility. *This concern might become increasingly challenging with a changing staffing situation, and the sudden loss of a key player may majorly disrupt partnership activity and even coherence. Plan for that inevitable eventuality.* With the best will in the world, there will be at least a small degree of attrition experienced. If it is only a few incidents, this is a strong indicator of high levels of investment and commitment to the partnership. It is essential to have someone in place with the role to meet schools when members of staff change, in order to keep momentum and buy-in. Continued involvement by the senior leaders is also important (even on an advisory only basis) and will often help to bolster flagging commitment.

It is an imperative, to conclude, that if any steering group is needed, it is established before substantive activities take place, so that it can closely monitor the actions of the partnership and advise on progress to ensure that delivery aligns with overall vision from the start. With the ELLI initiative, this role was carried out by researchers from the Eton Centre for Innovation and Research in Learning (CIRL), who interviewed all applicants to understand their motivations for taking part in the programme and their understanding of leadership. They sent surveys to all participants at the end of the programme which asked them to identify their perceived benefits from the programme and how the programme could improve, and conducted exit focus groups with students on free school meals to understand their perceived benefits of the programme. Finally, they collected data on academic outcomes from students who took part in the programme and compared that with those who did not. This enabled them to provide recommendations and key considerations for content, timetabling, and successful structures for collaboration and partnership across sectors. They also provided a proposed structure for other schools wishing to set up a leadership programme in their schools.

Evaluation

It's important to start by imagining what the desired measures of success are, *work out what that success should look like* and what the key ingredients are likely to be to get the programme there. It is then far easier to work backwards from that point. A brief, clear Theory of Change document can help to articulate what needs to be investigated, clarify what difference the partnership might want to make, and support the planning of activities that lead to the core outcomes. Measures of success will be dependent on what is being sought, but they do need to demonstrate with clarity how the intervention is going to make a difference, and how the series of connected activities undertaken might work together to make that difference. Good assessment measures need to be meaningful and appropriate, and should incorporate indicators which are easy to understand, realistic, appropriate to capture (against project and evaluative aims) and relatable to something genuinely measurable. *These indicators help to keep a logical 'line of sight' between the evaluative questions that need to be addressed and the provision of the measures of success and impact.* If the right questions are asked at the start, it sets the pattern throughout and ensures the right data are collected. It makes clear what the intended consequences are likely to be, and can therefore highlight what unintended consequences, both positive or negative, may have arisen. This is particularly significant when trying to ascertain whether any changes seen across a cohort or school can be correctly attributed to their active involvement over the lifetime of the project (although bearing in mind that it is an almost impossible task to disaggregate the specific effect of any one project from other supportive activities). Potential indicators could include 'distance travelled' with different data collection mechanisms for each question: surveys, tests, observations, interviews, small focus groups, question banks designed to capture attitudes, opinions, values, behaviour, or factual related information benefit the future of the partnership. There is also the danger of assuming that because the partnership in question has an assessment scheme, it necessarily means the partnership is working well. The monitoring of the success of partnerships is key, and despite the testing-fatigue across the teaching profession, a good programme is the one that continually asks itself how well it is doing and what might be changed to improve it in subsequent years.

To summarise, thought needs to be given in advance to the type of iterative research design to be employed. It should allow for flexibility to shape the research according to what is learnt from each stage, thus aiming to capitalise on every possible learning opportunity. With the ELLI initiative, in order to assess the impact, the CIRL looked at the character development of students by measuring their attitudes towards kindness (Binfet et al., 2016), humility (Krumrei-Mancuso and Rouse, 2016), respect, (Hjerm et al., 2020), integrity (Ingerson, 2014), and tolerance (Thomae et al., 2016) using standardised scales. They looked at the academic attainment of students on free school meals (FSM) by contrasting A-level and end-of-year exams (Year 12), and it was shown that the students who took part in ELLI performed better in their A-level results and comparable end-of-year exams. They were also accepted at elite universities. With regards to university destinations, 16% of the overall ELLI cohort went to Oxbridge compared to 12% of the overall cohort and 90% of ELLI students went to Russell Group universities (including Oxbridge) compared to 71% of the overall cohort.

Other partnerships

Alongside our partner schools, the LAE has close connections with a number of other providers. James Allen's Girls School, for example, have historically provided support for Oxford and Cambridge applicants, while Francis Holland School work closely with the Psychology Department to share best practice. Most recently, the LAE has been working with Putney High School to support the delivery of our increasingly-popular Philosophy, Religion and Ethics A-level course.

We also have a strong relationship with the Sutton Trust, the Fulbright Commission and a number of universities, including Oxford, Cambridge and King's College London. These relationships enable our sixth formers to take part in summer schools, including opportunities abroad, such as at Harvard University, Massachusetts. We are also able to provide sixth formers with many prestigious work experience opportunities through our governors, partner schools and their alumni.

To conclude, the voices of the Headteachers involved with the LAE say it all so much more effectively than the writers of this book ever could. Let's give them the last word in this chapter.

Headteachers' testimonials

Caterham School's relationship with the LAE has been transformational for our school and our community. As so often, a project designed to transform the lives of others has been the catalyst for positive change in ourselves. I hope, along the way, Caterham has also contributed to the excellence to be found in every corner of the LAE. My teaching colleagues have found inspiration in their interactions with an incredibly energising cohort of pupils which has rippled back into classrooms here at Caterham, and some of the solutions and learning we have had to develop to overcome the challenges of distance have also been impactful on teaching and learning practice here at Caterham. Partnership work is about more than just outcomes— it is also about appreciating the value, potential and expertise of different groups of people. This is a two-way process and I know that pupils here at Caterham have benefitted immensely from their interactions with their peers in Caterham House at the LAE. The culture of the LAE is one of high ambition and expectation underpinned by care for the individual—there is a proactive culture of wellbeing (underpinning incredible academic success) that we should all be incredibly proud of. The most significant impact our relationship with the LAE has had is on whole school culture here at Caterham—our commitment to using education as a vehicle to transform the trajectories and inspire the minds of young people no matter what their context—has given this school a purpose beyond exam results and has brought an ambition and energy to who we are, which continues to grow through our relationship with the LAE.

Caterham School – Ceri Jones, Headmaster

Eton's involvement in East London goes back to the Eton Mission to Hackney in the 19th century: the church of St Mary of Eton still stands within a mile of the LAE site in Stratford. A sign is still visible on the Lea Navigation pointing out the Eton Manor rowing club:

and the so-called 'Wilderness', the Eton Manor playing fields, offered transformational sporting opportunities to young people across East London until the 1960s.

Our involvement with the LAE is therefore absolutely in keeping with our historic work in East London, and one of the most rewarding aspects of our engagement has lain in reconnecting with those historic impulses. Our partnership has also returned Eton to its roots, as set out in its founding Charter of 1440, which establishes Eton as an education charity, one centred on a boys' boarding school in the Thames Valley, but not limited to that alone.

It is to this end that (at the time of writing) we have bid to government to open three new schools on the model of LAE—selective, small, sixth form colleges, with a laser-like focus on transforming the lives of the brightest and most Disadvantaged students. If our bid is successful, these schools will open in Oldham, on Teesside and in Dudley between 2025 and 2027, taking the LAE model of education and making it scalable and available to ever more young people who will benefit. I think it is fair to say that our involvement with the LAE project has had a profound impact on Eton as an institution, as well as on countless young East Londoners.

Eton College – Simon Henderson, Head Master

The starting point for partnerships is to create a means to share best practice, raise aspirations, and ensure that as many young people as possible can benefit from the sort of opportunities for personal development and academic achievement on offer at Forest. We were one of LAE's founding partner schools and have worked closely to support them since 2013 to see LAE become one of the highest-performing academic state sixth forms in the United Kingdom. At the outset we focused on setting up a hugely successful university application systems and offered guidance on co-curricular provision and currently host the LAE's Combined Cadet Force; we share events, pupil symposiums, lectures, staff training; we host LAE events here at Forest and enjoy pupil partnership with LAE's Forest House, while also currently supporting with safeguarding, mental health first aid, policy compliance and governance. LAE's determination to be a school where scholarship can flourish, where teaching comes from highly qualified subject specialists, and where access to top universities is available to all students, regardless of background, is the reason Forest wants to remain part of the driving force behind this astonishing school.

Forest School – Marcus Hodges, Warden

Highgate had long hoped for the opportunity to get involved in the governance of a school, seeing opportunity in founding an organisation which would mobilise the financial, intellectual and personnel capital of independent schools, for the good of the wider community. The LAE project has allowed us to do just that. On setting up LAE and indeed providing its founding Head, allowed Highgate to learn how to start a new venture, see which ideas work and which don't and understand the local 11–16 and community context. This meant that when the opportunity arose to do something similar in Tottenham, we were ready to jump at it; LAE in Stratford, both in its leadership team and governing body, was instrumental in getting our Tottenham LAE off the ground and the relationship has grown and strengthened ever since.

LAEs can attract academically-minded graduates to teaching and to introduce them and established teachers to highly aspirational, motivated and intelligent pupils, who may not hitherto have had that precious opportunity—with transformative results. I continue to hope that other schools will look at this model and convince themselves, their governors and their local partners that they can do the same: this can only be a good thing.

Highgate School – Adam Pettitt, Head

The concept was compelling. How could anybody not believe in offering ambitious, bright young people from Disadvantaged backgrounds the opportunity of an enriched sixth form experience from which to launch into the best universities in the land? UCS staff and pupils alike have enjoyed the mutual benefit of working in a variety of different ways with the colleagues and students of LAE. Such collaborations are fun, engaging and affirming, and bring about professional and personal development for all involved. Looking to the year ahead as an example, UCS anticipates continuing to share best practice on applications to Higher Education, organising further Public Speaking opportunities and Drawing Workshops, and hopes to extend our Music Collaboration. And the UCS–LAE House Visit and collaboration is always a highlight, with pupils from both schools enjoying the opportunity to meet, chat and compare notes. We have also benefitted from attending the LAE Careers Fair, and staff from the respective institutions are working together on how further to embed their careers programmes. Finally, to the heart of so much of what we all do, fellow teachers seem never to get enough of sharing ideas on teaching and learning – how lovely to have an entire other school's teaching body with whom to chew the pedagogical cud.

University College School Hampstead – Mark Beard, Headmaster

References

Binfet, J. T., Gadermann, A. M., and Schonert-Reichl, K. A. (2016) Measuring kindness at school: psychometric properties of a School Kindness Scale for children and adolescents. *Psychology in the Schools*, *53*, 111–126.

Hjerm, M., Eger, M. A., Bohman, A., and Connolly, F. F. (2020) A new approach to the study of tolerance: conceptualizing and measuring acceptance, respect, and appreciation of difference. *Social Indicators Research*, *147*, 897–919.

Ingerson, M.-C. (2014) Integrity matters: construction and validation of an instrument to assess ethical integrity as an attitudinal phenomenon. *Theses and Dissertations*, 5491. Available at: https://scholarsarchive.byu.edu/etd/5491 (accessed 23/07/2023).

Krumrei-Mancuso, E. J., and Rouse, S. V. (2016) The development and validation of the Comprehensive Intellectual Humility Scale. *Journal of Personality Assessment*, *98*, 209–221.

Thomae, M., Birtel, M. D., and Wittemann, J. (2016) The Interpersonal Tolerance Scale (IPTS): scale development and validation. Paper presented at the Annual Meeting of the International Society of Political Psychology, Warsaw, Poland, 13–16 July.

9
Fifteen Strategies to Drive 'Greater Expectations'

At the time of writing, the impact of the Covid-19 pandemic and the subsequent cost of living crisis have unleashed a series of profound shocks on already vulnerable communities, disrupting carefully constructed but fragile ecosystems of survival. This is in addition to the UK having experienced an extended decade-long crisis in social mobility, with a major attainment gap between students from the most and the least advantaged backgrounds stubbornly persisting. The Education Endowment Foundation (2018) has found that Disadvantaged learners are already over four months behind their more advantaged peers by the time they start at primary school. The gap then continues to widen as students progress through education, and has increased to over 19 months by the end of secondary school. Those from privileged backgrounds are significantly over-represented in the country's top professions and the most prestigious universities. Many of these disparities, which have life-long consequences, emerge in school (Lampl, 2018). Examining how well highly able students from Disadvantaged backgrounds perform academically is vital when trying to understand the inequalities in outcomes for these students further down the line, including their under-representation at leading universities and in the top professions (Kirby, 2016; Cullinane and Montacute, 2017). Schools or colleges can provide essential defences to prevent students' wellbeing and aspirations being swept away. To do so, inclusive school procedures need to be honed, secured and shared to more effectively support learners who face difficulty on a day-to-day basis. But what can schools do on a practical level? The Sutton Trust came to a depressing conclusion: 'Very little is currently known as to how to best support and stretch the highly able, especially those who are from lower socioeconomic backgrounds' (Montacute, 2018:4).

Fortunately, we disagree. We work with many educational institutions that have developed outstanding strategies, and their success is clear. But unfortunately, these successes are far too rarely shared or celebrated across the educational community. So in this chapter we have pulled together a shortlist of strategies that the LAE has developed and found to be effective in meeting the needs of our most able and Disadvantaged students.

Destigmatise disadvantage

A student's eligibility for free school meals (FSM) during their secondary education is a crude substitute for a scrupulous accounting of household means. Unlike the Income Deprivation Affecting Children Index (IDACI), which is a continuous, community-level variable, FSM eligibility is a binary measure related, in most cases, to receipt of social security benefits. Among those who qualify for FSM are young people whose families 'dip' into hardship and those who suffer endemic, even intergenerational poverty; among those who do not—in educational parlance, 'Other' students—can be counted young people from some of the poorest communities in the country but whose parents' immigration status excludes them from the benefits system, and also those students whose families enjoy six-figure incomes. Perhaps the best that can be said for FSM eligibility is that it is a consistent, if imperfect, measure of disadvantage that all schools have sufficient resources to track. This is not a small benefit. Notably, this degree of consensus around a single measure is wholly absent from the higher education sector in the UK.

The LAE has, for many years, proactively encouraged students and their families to register their eligibility for free school meals, and to destigmatise that status in and around school. The school leadership is very clear in its mission and communicates proactively with applicants and their families that the LAE will prioritise applications from those students in the greatest need. Students' first assembly in Year 12 often begins by pointing out those in attendance who have been eligible for free school meals, including the current Headteacher, at least one Governor and several members of the teaching faculty. The LAE also surveys students at the beginning of Year 12 to understand how long they have been eligible for free school meals. In such an environment, there is certainly less shame about poverty or difficulties, a clearer understanding of what others in the cohort are dealing with and less embarrassment about claiming for entitlements and support. There is also the clear advantage that students who know they are part of a majority will recognise the success of their peers as something they can emulate.

Guide, rather than pitch, when recruiting students

The LAE routinely receives more than 5,000 initial applications for what are currently just 250 available places in Year 12. Successful applicants can take comfort in knowing that they have been successful in an application process as competitive as almost any in the university sector. It would be easy to regard this tsunami of applications merely as a logistical hurdle to be overcome, but this would be a mistake. Any popular and successful school or college has an opportunity to use its recruitment process to provide high-quality information and guidance to applicants and their families.

The LAE's process includes clear signposting of career pathways to which students might aspire, along with healthy reassurance that most students will not yet know which career is right for them. Teachers who lead the school's pathways into medicine, law, engineering and finance run online guidance sessions, as do those responsible for Oxford and Cambridge applications and applications to international universities. The sessions increasingly feature the active involvement of LAE alumni working in the fields under discussion. Holding the sessions online makes scheduling more flexible, reduces staff workload and allows applicants to attend as many or as few sessions as they choose. The sessions are held *before* provisional offers are made, so that as many students as possible can access guidance. All students require guidance and support to choose the right A-level courses that will ensure a successful transition onto the most competitive university courses or other meaningful destinations. The purpose of this guidance is not to stream students early on, but to combat widely and firmly held misunderstandings about the relationship between A-level choice, degree and university selection, and eventual career goals. In an environment where a substantial minority of applicants will lack any direct exposure to the careers to which they aspire, there is an opportunity to make a profound contribution to the lives of many more students than will ever actually attend the school.

Get to know students as well as possible, as soon as possible

Sixth form schools or colleges often find issues around family-specific disadvantage harder to identify than the schools that their students have come from. They don't have the many years of accumulated experience with that child or the family and community that secondary schools typically do. Without investing the time with previous schools, there is a real danger that all that accumulated knowledge will be lost or delayed irretrievably. Sixth forms need to hit the ground running as they have less than two years to make their impact. If more information is shared at the start of the transition period, it ensures a far better starting point for more Disadvantaged students. This can be supplemented with a one-to-one interview or survey of new students. A suitably well-crafted interview or survey will throw up all types of issues. We must not expect our more Disadvantaged students to come forward with details of what is happening at home. Perhaps these issues are to do with refugee status, unemployment or imprisonment. Other issues can range from sudden family death to not having suitable shoes for interviews or the fare to get there. Sharing bedrooms, electricity turned off, meals bypassed and younger siblings to be cared for are also regular barriers to home studies, as is the spectre of homelessness and destitution. These can all too easily become the quietly assimilated shame of poverty. Many students from the poorest backgrounds do not necessarily see schools or colleges as a natural sanctuary to go to, particularly to address their family issues around finance. So interviews, conducted with sensitivity, will reveal far more of these issues than any more generic survey of student need. As a further practical step towards that identification of need, the LAE has developed its own Vulnerability Survey, which is supported by a wide range of evidence collected both before and after students are enrolled. Targeted support, specific funding and adapted practices at the school can then more easily follow.

Establish hard work as a basic expectation

Students aspiring to the most rewarding professions need to understand that they will be stretched—not in a way that jeopardises their wellbeing, but in a way that raises their potential. Sixth form schooling should prepare them for those demands. In addition, students who come from Disadvantaged backgrounds often have more ground to cover in the final years of their secondary education than students who have enjoyed greater opportunities earlier on. Finally, the sixth form experience is short, lasting barely more than five school terms. For all of these reasons, it is vital that the highest expectations are established right from the outset.

It needs to be stressed that all students are full-time students on an A-level programme of study, and in addition they must also have timetabled lessons for study skills, lectures, careers guidance and interventions. Prior to these new students applying, they need to be aware that the school or college day runs from 8 am to 6 pm, so the school or college needs to specify that students need to be onsite between these hours. This is one of the more challenging issues to be faced as many state school students tend to assume the school day ends at 3.30 pm. Some will assume that when they attend sixth form, their workload lightens (with free periods, etc.) and they can go home during this 'free time'. However, the expectation should be that these free periods are for working or undertaking co-curricular activities, sports, outreach and community engagement.

The LAE school week includes five hours of lessons in each A-level subject, an hour of study skills and an EPQ (Extended Project Qualification), lectures and other forms of academic enrichment, three hours of sports and other co-curricular activities and community outreach, and two hours of careers and university preparation. All students should be expected to undertake significant home learning to supplement their classroom studies. An extended curriculum means that students' study programmes should far exceed (by at least a third) government expectations for 16–19 study programmes, which are typically delivered in 600 hours. Online courses should be a key area for students to both catch up (subject-specific academic literacy) or be more fully stretched (subject-specific challenging enrichment and extension).

Teach the subject, not the specification

All schools and colleges encourage their students to achieve excellent academic results and to make positive progress throughout their time at school, but there is a level beyond this: a deliberate process of preparing students for what those A-level subjects will be like when studied at university. A-level exam specifications are the product of careful deliberation and intense work by skilled professionals. Inevitably, however, they involve subjective decisions about what to include and what to omit, compromise regarding scope and level of challenge, and idiosyncratic assessment features that can sometimes seem far removed from the subject proper. No school can ignore the specification or trust to the belief that able, productive students will do well with or without clear guidance regarding assessment protocols. But schools whose mission includes sending students to the most prestigious universities in the UK and elsewhere must address the fact that those universities expect applicants to have explored their chosen subjects far beyond the scope and demands of any exam. Schools concerned with the development of scholarship and a genuine love of learning should also be actively teaching young people that learning is valuable even where it is not formally assessed. Teachers should be encouraged to construct curricula around the explicit teaching of the threshold concepts that give coherence and integrity to the subject proper, regularly to go beyond the specification in terms of taught content, and to incorporate undergraduate materials in teaching at least for the most able in Year 13, but arguably also for all students. A carefully designed series of additional academic enrichment courses should be created that incorporate what we know to be good practice. It is a way to direct resources at those who will benefit most as well as giving teaching staff a clear idea of which students might benefit from further challenge in the classroom.

Normalise university-style learning

Attending lectures is a required part of university life, much though some students might think otherwise. Sixth formers need to grow comfortable with attending lectures and the style of learning that requires. A valuable contribution to students' development, which is also a relatively easy win, consists in establishing a programme of high-challenge lectures that should run weekly throughout the autumn and spring terms. These can be live, remote or recorded. Schools should tailor lecture programmes to their students' needs and aspirations. As a minimum, lectures should cover academic, pastoral, university and careers topics, including a focus on financial management and expectations.

At the LAE, the lecture programme acts as a supplement rather than as a substitute to the classroom experience. Lecture topics are specifically chosen to enhance students' understanding of their subjects rather than to consolidate or reinforce topics that have been covered in lessons. Where possible, lecturers are encouraged to draw connections across subjects and to emphasise the real-world relevance of academic topics. Lectures are often delivered by members of the teaching faculty, an experience that most teachers enjoy, which enhances their sense of their own scholarship and which encourages students to see their teachers in a new light. Lectures can also, of course, be drawn from outside school. LAE lectures are routinely delivered by working academics, independent scholars and professionals whose expertise lies in fields to which its students aspire, such as the law, medicine or engineering.

Provide extensive co-curricular opportunities

A-level study can be intense and the mountain of attainment that some students must climb to achieve a place at a good university is often daunting. Some school leaders have understandably responded by narrowing the focus of post-16 education to what they regard as 'core' activity, which is typically taken to mean lessons in three chosen subjects. The relative underfunding of post-16 education has only exacerbated this trend. But the LAE was founded on the conviction that this preference for narrowness was mistaken and that active involvement in co-curricular activity would support, rather than detract from, student achievement. Moreover, the provision of high-quality co-curricular activities are an essential way in which schools can help to address the gap in experience and education between those students whose parents can afford to pay for music lessons, language tuition, sports and many other things besides, and those who cannot. At the LAE, all students take part in sport or other physical activity, in clubs and societies, and devote time to community service. Every staff member is expected to contribute something to the co-curricular programme, whether it is yoga classes, football coaching or circus skills. And of course, the school benefits from its links with partner independent schools who have centuries' worth of combined experience of offering rich, life-enhancing co-curricular programmes.

Track performance forensically

Almost all schools these days are data rich, but not all schools are data enriched. Some school leaders have mapped the output of national datasets too directly onto individual students' performance as a blunt way of securing teacher accountability. By contrast, some teachers remain sceptical of the relevance of *any* objective dataset to the education of specific students. Neither position is constructive. The risks of both data misuse and data dismissiveness are particularly acute when addressing educational disadvantage. While it is true, to paraphrase Tolstoy, that each Disadvantaged family is Disadvantaged in its own way, this is more a question of idiosyncrasy than of novelty. Educational disadvantage results from a series of causes, most of them arising from or exacerbated by poverty, and often felt over several generations. These causes can and should be identified as potential sources of vulnerability, but must not be mistaken for predictors of underachievement. Schools committed to the constructive use of data to enhance achievement will track many, if not all, of the dimensions captured in the LAE Index of Need and will compare this analysis to large datasets where these are available. The LAE uses ALPS (Advanced Level Performance) Connect to measure how its students do relative to their peers with similar characteristics in other high-performing schools. Responsible school leaders will treat group comparison as the first stage of a meaningful analysis of student achievement and as a guide to any outcomes that seem anomalous. (Statisticians will rightly rail against assumed correlations between national datasets composed of several thousand students and groups measured in the tens or dozens.) They will also suspend judgement about the causes and character of those anomalies until several more stages of analysis have been performed to achieve a rounded understanding of what is driving an individual student's results. And they will do so routinely throughout a student's journey through the school.

'Keep up' beats 'catch up'

Schools can take too much comfort from the observation that, nationally, students who are Disadvantaged tend to make progress later in their A-level studies than other students. This is true, but can lead to the second half of Year 13 becoming something of a loaded bet on effective revision and last-minute intervention. It also risks conflating the gap in attainment between groups for a difference in each group's proximity to a specific point on the assessment curve. A-level grades, like any system of standardised assessment, have a limit factor. Some students—for example, those applying for the top universities and medical schools—will comfortably exceed that limit factor, while others may 'just' tip into it (while in no way meaning to undervalue these students' achievement). This is why information about destinations should be tracked alongside grades to ensure that the socioeconomic gradient is genuinely being flattened. Having established the systems and processes necessary to regularly analyse student achievement, schools should proactively target the highest levels of achievement for students from all backgrounds as early as possible in their sixth form education—albeit in a way that is compatible with their wellbeing. By no means does all this activity need to take the form of 'extra' intervention. The Education Endowment Foundation Framework, which emphasises in-class provision over out-of-class provision, is instructive here. At the LAE, the Disadvantage FIRST approach (which is detailed in Chapter 2) is a way of signposting the needs to make specific, informed provision for students whose home circumstances pose barriers to their academic achievement.

Embrace and celebrate academic excellence

Highly academic schools should unashamedly celebrate and should provide visible rewards for academic achievement. Contrary to the prevailing narrative in maintained schools, this sentiment is not in any way incompatible with celebrating other forms of achievement, nor should it lead inevitably to the emergence of an academic hierarchy. At the LAE, scholarships are offered both for absolute and for contextual achievement. Absolute grades matter, of course—particularly when scholarships are linked to achievement in specific subjects, such as mathematics or one of the modern foreign languages the school offers. But progress from a student's given baseline also matters and is celebrated in the form of whole school scholarships. The majority of LAE scholarships go to students who are Disadvantaged and are based on the trajectory of their achievement while in the sixth form. These scholarships are celebrated in assemblies, through school periodicals, in the form of letters home and in a variety of other conventional ways.

Scholars enjoy high visibility in the school community through specific badges and other identifiers. In the past, the LAE has experimented with the sorts of quasi-pecuniary rewards that have become common in state schools. More recently, the school leadership has concluded that these rewards are incompatible with the culture of scholarship the school seeks to foster. These days, scholarships entitle students to attend a residential trip devoted to the development of higher-level academic achievement and to broadening career aspirations.

... and excellence of all kinds

Academic scholarships should be balanced by the conscious development of a culture that celebrates active engagement across a range of other fronts. At the LAE, this takes the form of an LAE Diploma, which can be awarded for achievement in competitions, participation in outreach, leadership and service. These could include non-cognitive and employability skills and clubs and societies, web design, volunteering for local social activities, work discovery, the Duke of Edinburgh scheme and support for academic literacy or mentoring within school or college. Independent work could include an extended piece of writing based on wider ('super-curricular') reading, a detailed report about relevant work experience, submitting an essay to a relevant external essay competition, listening to and reporting back on subject-related podcasts, undertaking a MOOC (massive open online course), writing reviews of films in the language you want to study or subscribing to a topical journal or magazine. Together, these activities can contribute to an internally recognised diploma. Working towards a diploma should help to cultivate an ethos of independent thinking, self-discipline, communication, confidence, and teamwork. Some schools or colleges have an awards ceremony akin to the Oscars. All students attend in black tie/ball gowns, etc., and, for the big awards, students are required to prepare mini acceptance speeches (similar to a one-to-three-minute valedictorian speech).

Invest in university preparation

Create a course, starting as early as possible in the autumn term of Year 12, that supports students to make well-informed choices regarding university courses and destinations that match their achievement and interests. Clarify the immediate timeline, how the process works, actions to take now to start building a personal profile for university and employment and careers guidance. Introduce what A-level subjects will be like when they are studied at university and give students the tools for deepening their understanding for A-level subjects and beyond.

Encourage students to aspire to the top universities and high-tariff courses and the best degree apprenticeships, high-tariff courses and the best degree apprenticeships. The pathway should lead students through the application process, and ensure they have the subject knowledge and academic language they will need to access the university courses with confidence. Courses should include tuition on study habits, self-management skills, prioritising, independent study and time management, all of which they will need to thrive once they are at university. The pathway should be more than a preparation for university, however; it will need to be designed to create a broad and deep intellectual experience that values high aspirations. Students should increasingly encounter learning as an independent and interdependent experience through academic integrity and scholarship, intellectual curiosity and criticality, struggle, risk-taking and autonomy, self-regulation and self-awareness, and depth and mastery.

Establish dedicated routes into Oxbridge, medical schools and international universities

We don't have to accept any simple hierarchy of universities, with their almost unavoidable overtones of snobbery, to acknowledge that some universities have quite distinct entry requirements and processes. Schools with substantial numbers of students who sincerely aspire to attend those universities need to prepare those students appropriately. In a typical year, the LAE sends between 10% and 15% of its students to Oxbridge and roughly the same percentage to medical schools. While there are third-party organisations and websites that can be useful sources of information, university access on this scale requires dedicated in-school resourcing. And there is, unfortunately, something to the argument that those best placed to facilitate access to specific universities, or types of university, are likely to be graduates of those universities. The LAE has an Oxford and Cambridge Coordinator who runs a year-long programme: first, to encourage students of all backgrounds with the right academic profile to apply to one or another of those universities; then to guide those students carefully through the choice of course and college that is right for them; and finally to work with the wider team of tutors and House leaders to manage students' mental wellbeing throughout the process of application. The school's Medicine, Dentistry and Veterinary (MDV) Coordinator runs a 'Pathways to Medicine' programme of lectures, interview preparation and application workshops aimed at providing the same level of support. The school's International Universities Coordinator performs a similar role in supporting students applying to universities in the United States and in the European Union, although fewer students opt for this route. In the specific case of applications to Ivy League universities in the USA, working closely with the Sutton Trust has proven to be essential. Departments are responsible for providing admissions testing preparation, interview practice and personal statement advice.

Focus on informed, impartial careers education

All students should receive effective information, advice and guidance to support them in making choices that will enhance their life chances, guide them in choosing career paths that suit their interests and abilities, and help them to sustain employability throughout their working lives. More Disadvantaged students may have far fewer role models that they can emulate and are likely to have experienced family unemployment, sometimes generational unemployment. Students should receive a rich provision of careers education, both inside the classroom, online and within professional contexts, in accordance with the eight Gatsby Benchmarks. The key elements of a successful careers programme are:

1   the identification and cultivation of skills and competencies that have broad applicability across sectors and professions
2   regular exposure to people working in the fields to which students aspire

At the LAE, the first of these elements is rooted in the school's Career Essentials, developed in partnership with major employers representing the sectors in which LAE alumni most often work. The second element is evident in an active mentoring and Pathways programme that puts students in touch with working professionals across a variety of industry sectors. This programme should include internship and work experience opportunities, as well as sessions on how to network and make a good impression when students are on them. Most Disadvantaged students will not have family contacts to ensure good work experience and so schools or colleges need to establish and share links with industry. Finally, as a practical matter, many students from low-income homes need to work outside term time during their A-level studies. Industry partners need to be educated in the value of paid rather than unpaid internships in order to democratise access to certain types of professional learning.

Stay close to alumni

Perhaps maintaining close relationships with school alumni has become quite standard practice in many independent schools, but it is far rarer, yet more significant and necessary, in Disadvantaged schools and colleges. There should be a focus on staying close to the students who were originally designated as having free school meals (FSM) or in Looked After Children (LAC), who then made it to top universities. How did they manage it? Did they then manage that university transition well? What really helped them? How did they transition beyond those institutions? What measures that the school or college put in place supported them the most? Obviously sixth form schools and colleges need to acknowledge their role in this success, but the alumni also have a responsibility to give feedback to the schools who put in so much time and effort earlier in those students' academic life. The trickle-down of these success stories help to boost and restore communities. They also help to encourage role modelling that is so significant. Those students can also be recruited to give back to younger students in terms of interview practice, CV preparation and admission statements. The impact of such things cannot be underestimated— someone from that community, with those Disadvantaged labels, who has defeated the odds, sharing what strategies helped them to do it.

Conclusion

Throughout its first decade, the LAE has tried to support students' aspirations without sacrificing their wellbeing. No list of strategies aimed at such an ambitious goal can hope to be definitive. The strategies detailed above have all played a part in the school's success. We believe they can contribute to the success of other schools and other students operating and learning in different contexts. Some of these strategies may seem daunting, depending on colleagues' context. 'Normalising university style learning' will seem very far removed from the day-to-day experience of teachers and school leaders working in communities with very low rates of participation in higher education over multiple generations. Nonetheless, most of the suggestions above are practical and within the reach of most, if not all, schools. We have used the term 'strategies' to follow the convention in schools, but a reader familiar with corporate strategy development would likely call many of the suggestions 'tactics' and this might better reflect the practical nature of many of our suggestions.

Scale is undoubtedly a factor. Although a small school, the LAE has a concentration of high-achieving students who might otherwise be spread over several dozen secondary schools or a handful of sixth form colleges. But schools do not have to go it alone: whether through multi-academy trusts, local authority systems or looser federations and partnerships, schools may find it easier to implement many of the recommended strategies by working together. Above all, schools should de-stigmatise disadvantage and recognise the potential that is to be found in young people from all backgrounds and personal circumstances. Contrary to the Sutton Trust—an organization that we nonetheless admire greatly—we believe that the sort of education that is most likely to propel students from all backgrounds to the richest, most rewarding universities and careers is readily identifiable and, with time, patience and skill, eminently replicable.

References

Cullinane, C., and Montacute, R. (2017) *Fairer Fees: Reforming Student Finance to Increase Fairness and Widen Access*. London: The Sutton Trust. Available at: www.suttontrust.com/wp-content/uploads/2019/12/Fairer-Fees-Final.pdf (accessed 23/07/2023).

Education Endowment Foundation (EEF) (2018) *The Attainment Gap*. London: EEF. Available at: https://educationendowmentfoundation.org.uk/support-for-schools/bitesize-support/closing-the-attainment-gap (accessed 23/07/2023).

Kirby, P. (2016) *Leading People: The Educational Backgrounds of the UK Professional Elite*. London: The Sutton Trust. Available at: www.suttontrust.com/wp-content/uploads/2019/12/Leading-People_Feb16-1.pdf (accessed 23/07/2023).

Lampl, P. (2018) Foreword. In R. Montacute, *Potential for Success: Fulfilling the Promise of Highly Able Students in Secondary Schools*. London: The Sutton Trust, p. 2. Available at: www.suttontrust.com/wp-content/uploads/2019/12/PotentialForSuccess.pdf (accessed 23/07/2023).

Montacute, R. (2018) *Potential for Success: Fulfilling the Promise of Highly Able Students in Secondary Schools*. London: The Sutton Trust. Available at: www.suttontrust.com/wp-content/uploads/2019/12/PotentialForSuccess.pdf (accessed 23/07/2023).

Afterword

From the glimmer of an idea to a thriving reality, during its first decade the LAE has established itself as one of the highest performing sixth form schools in the country in any sector.

Central to this achievement has been a steadfast belief in the importance of a generous and robust co-curriculum programme and a supportive and effective network of pastoral care. Great academic results grow from a genuinely holistic approach to education in which students value determination and curiosity and the excitement of new horizons. They value each other, too.

In the next decade, the LAE will focus on sharing this mindset and success with other state schools to the benefit of a wider range of students from Disadvantaged backgrounds through its strategic commitments to 'Celebrating Excellence, Sharing Excellence'.

Part of this extending reach will be seen in the LAE's move to its new building in 2025. This move will enable the school to increase its enrolment by 50%, with students drawn from all over East London. The school will also make its new facilities available out of hours to a variety of community groups so that it can contribute more widely to the progressive transformation of Stratford.

When it comes to identifying the young people who would benefit most from an LAE education, the school has developed its definition of socioeconomic disadvantage to adopt what is possibly the most progressive set of oversubscription criteria of any academically selective school in the country. As a consequence, the school has seen an increase of almost 60% in the number of applications from students who come from Disadvantaged backgrounds.

Conscious that there are many students who aspire to an LAE education but cannot be offered places, the school has reformed its procedures for recruiting students to provide destination advice of high quality to all its 5,500 applicants rather than only those to whom it makes formal offers.

The writing of this book has been a project aimed at showing through daily practice how a sixth form education of outstanding quality can be realised. In that spirit, the LAE will engage more directly with schools and students in parts of the country where opportunities are limited. One significant way to help is by enabling teachers from more challenging environments access to the LAE professional development programme. More direct engagement will include working closely with Eton Star Colleges in the North of England.

All our thinking and planning comes back to the experience of our students. In this next decade we will see ever more opportunities being created for alumni through the development of a dedicated alumni portal, through social media communities and through alumni events. We are keen to involve our alumni in the future of their school, through the gap year support staff programme, coming back as permanent members of the teaching staff (following the first such appointment in 2022) and, over time, recruiting alumni into governance roles.

In its short life, the LAE has developed the momentum and ambition to embed its values and ethos. The next decade will see expansion and growth, but the mission will remain the same—to give students broad and rich life choices in a complex and changing future.

Tony Little, Chair of Governors, The London Academy of Excellence

Index

Page numbers in **bold** indicate tables.

A-level programme, 31–3, 129–30
academic achievement, celebrating, 50–1, 132–3
academic interviews, for teaching posts, 69–70
academic literacy support, 32, 33, 133
academic partnership, 108
academic persuasion, 53–4
academic resilience, 51–2
academies programme, 2
admissions policy, 20–2, 127
agency, teacher, 59, 61–3
ALPS Connect, 131
alumni, 96, 98, 99, 100, 104, 127, 135, 136, 140
ambassadors, student, 78–82
anxious literalism, 43–4
aptitude test preparation, 96
Aristotle, 39
aspirations, students', 23–4, 30–1, 98–9, 127
assemblies, school, 84
autonomy, teacher, 59–61

BAME network, 83
Beard, Mark, 123
Berger, Ron, 11
Biesta, G. J. J., 65
bite-sized approaches, 46
boundedness of threshold concepts, 38–9
Brighton College, 102, 107, 111

Cambridge University
    applications to, 2, 87, 92, 93, 94, 95, 96,
        120, 127, 134
    partnership with, 120–1
care experience, **18**
career aspirations, 23–4, 30–1, 98–9, 127
careers education programme, 32, 97–105, 135
    aspirations and shifting preferences, 98–9
    mentoring programme, 82, 103–5, 135
    qualities essential for success, 99–103, **101**
    Career Essentials, 97–8, 100–3, **101**, 135
carer status, **18**
Caterham School, 107, 121
celebration of excellence, 50–1, 132–3

challenge strategies, 43–56
    accredit previous learning, 49–50
    base courses on threshold concepts, 46
    build in misconception tracking points, 49–50
    build positive academic resilience, 51–2
    celebrate scholarship, 50–1, 132–3
    clarify purpose and relevance of subject, 47
    expectation of hard work, 128–9
    focus on longer-term learning, 47–8
    model subject-specific academic language,
        38–9, 48–9
    offer feedback and redrafting, 53–4
    plan in complexity, debate and doubt, 54–5
    ratchet up task difficulty, 51–2
    teach to the top and go 'off piste', 52–3
character development, 102–3
    see also ELLI (Eton & London Academy
        of Excellence Leadership Institute)
        programme
Child in Need Plans, **18**
Child Protection Plans, **18**
CIRL *see* Tony Little Centre for Innovation and
    Research in Learning (CIRL), Eton
clubs and societies, 32, 33, 83, 85, 133
co-curricular partnership, 108
co-curricular programme, 32, 33, 82–3, 85,
    101–3, 129, 130–1, 133
co-teaching, 114
Collins, Jim, 68
community outreach programme, 32, 33, 129
concepts *see* threshold concepts
confusion endurance, 54–5
context principle, 7
continuous professional development *see*
    professional development
cooperative principle, 39
Counsell, Christine, 8, 9
counselling service, 77, 85–6
Covid-19 pandemic, 77, 79, 102, 125
cultural capital, 5, 37
culture of vigilance, 77
culture wars, 29–30

curriculum, 29–31
  A-level programme, 31–3, 129–30
  co-curricular programme, 32, 33, 82–3, 85,
    101–3, 129, 130–1, 133
  critical approaches, 29–30
  disadvantage and, 22–5
  expectation of hard work, 129–30
  LAE curriculum, 22–5, 31–3
  personal development, 82–4
  students' aspirations and, 23–4, 30–1
  teaching the subject, not the specification,
    129–30
  see also threshold concepts
curriculum partnership, 108

Davis, Miles, 62
deep structure of teaching and learning, 9–10,
  26, 110
development partnership, 108
disadvantage, 1–2, 15–27
  admissions policy and, 20–2
  curriculum and, 22–5
  destigmatising, 17–22, 126–7
  Disadvantaged FIRST approach, 25–6, **26**,
    132
  identifying and understanding need, 17–20,
    18, 126–8
  students' aspirations and, 23–4
Duke of Edinburgh scheme, 32, 133

Early Help provision planning, 85
ECO network, 83, 84
Education Endowment Foundation (EEF), 17, 19,
  26, 61, 125, 132
Education Healthcare Plans, **18**
educational disadvantage see disadvantage
ELLI (Eton & London Academy of Excellence
  Leadership Institute) programme, 111, 112,
  113, 114, 115, 116, 117–18, 119, 120
employability skills, 32, 97–8, 100–3, **101**, 133,
  135
English as an additional language (EAL), **18**, 21
environmental safeguarding, 87–8
EPQ (Extended Project Qualification), 32, 33, 129
ethic of excellence, 11
ethic of improvement, 53–4
ethnic minority status, **18**
Eton College, 61, 107, 121–2
  Tony Little Centre for Innovation and
    Research in Learning (CIRL), Eton, 115,
    119, 120
  see also ELLI (Eton & London Academy
    of Excellence Leadership Institute)
    programme
excellence, ethic of, 11
extended curriculum, 32, 129
  see also co-curricular programme

family disruption, **18**
feedback, **26**, 45, 53–4
female student voice, 75
Forest School, 102, 107, 111, 122
Francis Holland School, 120
free periods, 129
free school meals (FSM), 1, 3, 7, 16, **18**, 19,
  126–7
Free Schools, 2
Fulbright Commission, 120
Further Education Inspection Framework, 102
Futures Fair, 103

games programme, 32, 33
Gatsby Benchmarks, 100, 135
Gender Equality Network, 83
genericism, 9
Goethe, Johann, 6
Gorard, S. A. C., 19
grammar schools, 3, 19
Grice, Paul, 39

Hancock, Herbie, 62
hard work, expectation of, 128–9
Henderson, Simon, 121–2
Highgate School, 107, 123
Hodges, Marcus, 122
homelessness, **18**
household income, **18**

implicit structure of teaching and learning, 9
imposter syndrome, 36, 55, 73, 78
improvement, ethic of, 53–4
Income Deprivation Affecting Children Index
  (IDACI), 126
Independent and State School Partnership (ISSP)
  see partnership working
independent learning skills, 32, 94–5, 130
Index of Need, 17–20, **18**
innovation in teaching, 59, 62–3
integrative function of threshold concepts,
  37–8
International Universities Coordinator, 135
international university applications, 127, 135
interview practice, 96, 117
interviews, for teaching posts, 69–70
irreversible nature of threshold concepts, 39–40

James Allen's Girls School, 120
Jones, Ceri, 121

Keeping Children Safe in Education, 77
King's College London, 120–1

LAE see London Academy of Excellence (LAE)
Lambert, David, 29
Land, R., 34, 35

language
    English as an additional language (EAL), **18**, 21
    subject-specific academic language, 38–9, 48–9
    targeted support, **26**
leadership development *see* ELLI (Eton & London Academy of Excellence Leadership Institute) programme
learning
    independent, 32, 94–5, 130
    longer-term, 47–8
    see also teaching and learning
Learning Essentials, 58–9, 63–6, **64**
lecture programme, 95, 130
Leeds Beckett LGBTQ+ Inclusion in Education Award, 83
lesson observations, 66–7
'Levelling Up' agenda, 2
LGBTQ+ group, 83, 84
London Academy of Excellence (LAE), 2–4
    admissions policy, 20–2, 127
    alumni, 96, 98, 99, 100, 104, 127, 135, 136, 140
    co-curricular programme, 32, 33, 82–3, 85, 101–3, 129, 130–1, 133
    curriculum, 22–5, 31–3
    Disadvantaged FIRST approach, 25–6, **26**, 132
    Futures Fair, 103
    Index of Need, 17–20, **18**
    LAE Diploma, 33, 100, 101–3, 133
    Learning Essentials, 58–9, 63–6, **64**
    lecture programme, 95, 130
    mentoring programme, 82, 103–5, 135
    Pathways programme, 102, 103, 135
    performance tracking, 131
    scholarships, 86–7, 132–3
    school day/week, 128–9
    student recruitment, 20–2, 127
    see also careers education programme; challenge strategies; partnership working; safeguarding and support; teaching and learning; university preparation
London Borough of Newham, 20–1, 87
longer-term learning, 47–8

Markovits, Daniel, 4, 5
masterclasses, 95
Matthew effect, 6–7
medical school applications, 2, 87, 92, 93, 94, 95, 96, 127, 134–5
Medicine, Dentistry and Veterinary (MDV) Coordinator, 134–5
mental health issues, **18**
Mental Health Network (MHN), 79–82
mentoring, 78, 82, 103–5, 133, 135

meritocracy, 4
Meyer, J. H. F., 34, 35
misconception tracking points, 49–50
mock exams, 32
Montacute, R., 126

National Foundation for Educational Research (NFER), 59, 60
Need, Index of, 17–20, **18**
networks, student, 78–82, 83–4
non-cognitive skills, 32, 133

Oates, Tim, 34
Ofsted, 44–5, 63, 64, 102
Oxford and Cambridge Coordinator, 134
Oxford Poverty and Human Development Initiative, 17
Oxford University
    applications to, 2, 87, 92, 93, 94, 95, 96, 120, 127, 134
    partnership with, 120–1

parental education, **18**, 20
parents, students' aspirations and, 23–4, 98
partnership working, 107–23
    adaptation built in, 112–13
    benefits of, 108–10
    clarifying gains, 113–14
    evaluation, 119–20
    four quadrants of, 108
    headteachers' testimonials, 121–3
    meeting genuine needs, 116–17
    other partnerships, 120–1
    outcomes, 117–18
    scrutiny, 118–19
    trust, 114–16
    wider aims, 111–12
pastoral support *see* safeguarding and support
Pathways programme, 102, 103, 135
pedagogy, 57–71
    agency, 59, 61–3
    autonomy, 59–61
    Disadvantaged FIRST approach, 25–6, **26**, 132
    evidence of learning, 66–7
    expectation of hard work, 129–30
    independent learning skills, 32, 94–5, 130
    innovation, 59, 62–3
    Learning Essentials, 58–9, 63–6, **64**
    lesson observations, 66–7
    professional trust, 62–3
    recruiting for subject expertise, 68–70
    rigour, 59
    subject-specific, 8–10, 110, 129–30
    teaching the subject, not the specification, 129–30
    three dimensions of signature pedagogies, 8–9
    see also challenge strategies; threshold concepts

peer review, 54
perceived autonomy, 60
performance tracking, 131
perinatal factors, 19–20
personal development curriculum, 82–4
    see also co-curricular programme; ELLI
        (Eton & London Academy of Excellence
        Leadership Institute) programme
Personal Growth and Development club, 84
Pettitt, Adam, 123
physical health issues, **18**
physical home environment, 19–20
poverty *see* disadvantage
praise, **26**, 37, 52
Prevent risk assessment and training, 77
Priestley, M., 62
professional development, 57, 58
    partnership working and, 110, 113
    subject-specific pedagogy, 8–10, 110
    teacher agency and, 62–3
    see also staff training
Professional Skills and Competencies
    Framework, 100, **101**, 102–3, 135
professional trust, 62–3
Putney High School, 120

Quality First Teaching, 26

radicalisation, protecting students from, 77
recognition, Disadvantaged FIRST approach, **26**
recruitment
    student, 20–2, 127
    teacher, 68–70
recruitment training, 77
redrafting, 53–4
refugee status, **18**
relational safeguarding, 75, 87
resilience, academic, 51–2

safeguarding and support, 73–89
    counselling team, 77, 85–6
    embedded leadership of, 76–8, 88
    environmental safeguarding, 87–8
    importance of, 74–5
    Mental Health Network, 79–82
    personal development curriculum, 82–4
    relational safeguarding, 75, 87
    safeguarding culture and practice review, 87–8
    scholars' programme, 86–7, 132–3
    school assemblies, 84
    School Council, 86
    staff training, 76, 77
    student ambassadors, 78–82
    student networks, 78–82, 83–4
    student voice, 75
    vertical tutoring, 78
    wellbeing ambassadors, 79–82

Safeguarding Committee, 76
Safeguarding Governor, 76, 77, 86
Sandel, Michael, 4, 5
scaffolding, 37, 52
scholars' programme, 86–7, 132–3
scholarship, celebrating, 50–1, 132–3
school assemblies, 84
School Council, 86
school counselling team, 77, 85–6
school day/week, 128–9
seating, classroom, **26**
self-esteem, 51–2, 55
Selfology, 81
sex and relationships education, 85
Shoda, Y., 7
Shulman, L. S., 8–9
Siddiqui, N., 19
Simon, Herbert, 38
skills and competencies, 32, 97–8, 100–3, **101**,
    133, 135
social home environment, 19–20
social mobility, 1–2, 4–6
socioeconomic disadvantage *see* disadvantage
special educational needs and disability (SEND)
    status, 7, **18**, 21
staff surveys, 59, 113–14
staff training
    Prevent training, 77
    safeguarding, 76, 77
    safer recruitment training, 77
    see also professional development
Strand, S., 20
student ambassadors, 78–82
student aspirations, 23–4, 30–1, 98–9, 127
student destinations *see* careers education
    programme; university preparation
student networks, 78–82, 83–4
student recruitment, 20–2, 127
student surveys, 19, 22, 24, 31–2, 75, 77, 81–2,
    114, 119, 126, 128
student voice, 75
student wellbeing *see* safeguarding and support
subject-specific academic language, 38–9, 48–9
subject-specific pedagogy, 8–10, 110, 129–30
Sunday Times annual schools survey, 24
support *see* safeguarding and support
surface structure of teaching and learning, 9
surveys
    staff, 59, 113–14
    student, 19, 22, 24, 31–2, 75, 77, 81–2, 114,
        119, 126, 128
Sutton Trust, 120, 126, 135, 137

teacher agency, 59, 61–3
teacher autonomy, 59–61
teacher development *see* professional
    development; staff training

Teacher Development Trust, 59
teacher recruitment, 68–70
teaching and learning, 57–71
    agency, 59, 61–3
    autonomy, 59–61
    Disadvantaged FIRST approach, 25–6, **26**, 132
    evidence of learning, 66–7
    expectation of hard work, 129–30
    independent learning skills, 32, 94–5, 130
    innovation, 59, 62–3
    Learning Essentials, 58–9, 63–6, **64**
    lesson observations, 66–7
    professional trust, 62–3
    recruiting for subject expertise, 68–70
    rigour, 59
    subject-specific pedagogy, 8–10, 110, 129–30
    teaching the subject, not the specification,
        129–30
    three dimensions of signature pedagogies,
        8–9
    see also challenge strategies; threshold
        concepts
Teaching and Learning Handbook, 58–9
Teaching and Learning Toolkit, 61
Teaching Excellence Framework, 63, 94
testing, Disadvantaged FIRST approach, **26**
three dimensions of signature pedagogies, 8–9
threshold concepts, 33–41
    basing courses on, 46
    boundedness of, 38–9
    importance of, 34, 40–1
    integrative function of, 37–8
    irreversible nature of, 39–40
    transformative, 36–7, 46
    troublesome nature of, 35–6
Todd, Selina, 4, 5
Tony Little Centre for Innovation and Research
    in Learning (CIRL), Eton, 115, 119, 120

Toom, A., 61
training *see* staff training
transformative concepts, 36–7, 46
troublesome nature of threshold concepts, 35–6
trust
    in partnership working, 114–16
    professional, 62–3
tutoring, vertical, 78

UK Household Longitudinal Survey (UKHLS), 60
University College School Hampstead, 107, 123
university preparation, 32, 33, 92–6, 133–4
    aptitude test preparation, 96
    challenging truths about, 93
    course choice, 96
    independent learning skills, 32, 94–5, 130
    international university applications, 127, 135
    interview practice, 96, 117
    lecture programme, 95, 130
    masterclasses, 95
    normalising university experience, 93–5, 130
    Oxbridge and medical school applications,
        2, 87, 92, 93, 94, 95, 96, 120, 127,
        134–5
    partnership working and, 116–18, 120

vertical tutoring, 78
vigilance, culture of, 77
Vygotsky, Lev, 25

wellbeing *see* safeguarding and support
wellbeing ambassadors, 79–82
Wiliam, Dylan, 65
Willingham, D., 33
Wilshaw, Sir Michael, 44
work discovery programme, 32, 33, 133

Young, Michael, 4, 6, 10, 25, 29, 30, 68